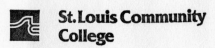

China's Traditional Rural Architecture

Ronald G. Knapp

China's Traditiona

 University of Hawaii Press • Honolulu

Rural Architecture

A Cultural Geography

of the Common House

Library of Congress Cataloging-in-Publication Data

Knapp, Ronald G.
   China's traditional rural architecture.

   Bibliography: p.
   Includes index.
   1.   Architecture, Domestic—China.   2.   Vernacular
architecture—China.   3.   Architecture, Domestic—Taiwan.
4.   Vernacular architecture—Taiwan.   I.   Title.
NA7448.K57   1986   728'.0951   86-7003
ISBN 0-8248-1053-8

To the memory of William Harry Knapp, Sr.,
and Thelma Weber Knapp

CONTENTS

Color plates follow page 114

PREFACE AND ACKNOWLEDGMENTS

GEOGRAPHERS have a long tradition of looking at houses, not only because dwellings figure prominently in any cultural landscape but because houses represent a structured expression of complex interrelationships linking people and environments as they vary across time and space. This study of China's traditional rural architecture is a preliminary effort at understanding the common rural house, placing it within its various physical and cultural environments. The book draws liberally from research in collateral social sciences, humanities, and technical fields.

Joseph Spencer published in 1947 the first exploratory examination by a geographer of the Chinese house. The insights provided in his short article later intrigued me in my early training as a geographer. His cautious approach in describing "the houses of the Chinese" across a nation that is as large as the United States and one with pronounced regional and subregional variation has guided me as I carried out my own ambitious research. His interest, like mine later, was with folk or vernacular dwellings, those of common peasants rather than the large dwellings of the wealthy that more obviously provide linkages with Chinese monumental architecture.

I first encountered Chinese rural dwellings when I went to Taiwan as a graduate student in 1965. Since then, virtually all my work has dealt in one way or another with the ways Chinese organize space at many levels, the house perhaps being the most fundamental. Taiwan in the mid-1960s was an island in transition, attempting to marry a traditional past to a dynamic future. Hasty development, however, sometimes brought with it forced and unsuitable change that denied the accumulated expertise of countless generations of peasants who generally well understood their environments. I recall being intrigued with the striking contrasts between the new and the old in rural housing patterns. In one instance, on the northern outskirts of Taibei in the middle of a paddy field, some new two-story row houses were being built to accommodate those leaving the city and those farmers who wished to live in modernized housing. At the end of most of the new narrow lanes were deteriorating nineteenth-century rural dwellings which like nearby temples all had a common directional orientation and a layout that mirrored traditional mainland patterns. The new housing, on the other hand, was oriented 90 degrees away from that of the rural houses, faced each other across streets, and had an interior layout that suggested Western garden apartments rather than Chinese social needs. These dichotomies in form and orientation puzzled me, leading eventually to a search for the meaning of the Chinese house and its transformations.

Some individuals contributed more directly than others to this research. Whether providing broad insights, specific comments and criticisms, technical knowledge or illustrative material, I am grateful to them all. Samuel C. Chu and Ray Huang, two historians, nurtured in me the need to see Chinese cultural patterns in historical perspective. Their own work also shows the mark of a broad disciplinary perspective. The art historian Hugo Munsterberg traveled with me twice to China. Listening to his elucidation of China's great monumental architecture heightened my sensitivity to recurrent patterns and symbolism. During the summer of 1984, I had the opportunity to participate in a seminar on traditional Chinese architecture at Qinghua University in Beijing. In the classroom and in the field, the Qinghua architectural staff and graduate students deepened my understanding of Chinese architecture from a Chinese perspective. I owe a great debt to Professor Wu Huanjia of Qinghua University's Department of Architecture for his willingness to share his knowledge and make it possible for me to go off on my own or with others to see those aspects of rural architecture that especially interested me. Throughout this period in Beijing, I was indeed fortunate to be with an American architect and good friend, John F. Meyer, A.I.A., whose experience and critical eye helped guide my own understanding of the structure and aesthetics of buildings.

The contributions of many others in many disciplines is apparent throughout the volume, in citations and in illustrations. Especially noteworthy are the photographs of Arthur J. Van Alstyne. Taking advantage of his lengthy stay in some areas of China I was not able to visit, he diligently recorded rural housing patterns that enrich the book. Others who were generous with illustrative material are Huang Hanmin of the Building Design Institute of Fujian Province; Paul Sun, A.I.A., of Boston whose special interest in gaining knowledge of Chinese traditional architecture has led to his organization of two Earthwatch expeditions to China; the anthropologist Lawrence Crissman, who visited with me from Australia to discuss my research and share some of his pictures of housing in Taiwan; and Leonard H. D. Gordon, the historian, whose single illustration of the modernization of pillar construction in Taiwan's dwellings filled a gap.

Many individuals read parts or the complete manuscript. I thank them for their care and suggestions for improvements. Two geographers, Christopher L. Salter and Arthur J. Van Alstyne, carefully read the entire text and offered not only corrections but good encouragement. Nancy Shatzman Steinhardt meticulously scrutinized the text, bringing the eye of an art historian to many details. Her own work on Chinese monumental architecture served as resource materials for me. I was fortunate in being able to draw on the expertise of two friends to clarify textual problems with Chinese historical materials. Jen-jen Hsu, an anthropologist, checked some of my translations and offered freely his own knowledge of the house as social symbol. Hua-tung Gordon Lee, an engineer very knowledgeable of China's classical language, sharpened not only my language but also understanding of a number of passages. Gary Seaman, an anthropologist who is carrying out research on Chinese geomancy, took on the task of evaluating the chapter on Chinese folk religion and the built environment. His comments on this chapter have found their way into some of the others. It is clear that collectively their comments and criticisms have helped improve the argument and presentation of *China's Traditional Rural Architecture*. The shortcomings that remain are my own.

The photographs found throughout the book were largely taken by me on more than a dozen trips to the China mainland and Taiwan over the past twenty years, with most of them taken since 1977. Special thanks are owed Daisy Yau, vice-president of Inter Pacific Tours International, who not only made it possible for me to spend time in Tibet, Xinjiang, Yunnan, and Gansu but also longer than normal periods in the more frequently visited parts of the country. Some of the illustrations are from Chinese sources; all have been acknowledged. Many of these have been improved by Camy Fischer, an artist, who was able to take some of my sketches and ideas and make them presentable.

Not the least, I owe a great deal to my wife May and children Larissa and Jeffrey who often had an absent husband and father while this book was in progress, whether I was in China, at the library, or at my PC.

Preliminary support for research on rural housing in Taiwan was provided in 1977 by an Association of American Geographers grant. Similar support for mainland patterns was provided in 1979–1980 from the State University of New York Research Foundation. However, the research would not have been as complete or as swift if it had not been for the National Endowment for the Humanities whose fellowship made it possible for me to carry out full-time research and writing during calendar year 1984. The assistance of the State University of New York, College at New Paltz, is gratefully acknowledged.

The editorial support of the University of Hawaii Press has been consistent. The task of creating a book which involves not only textual but abundant illustrative material put substantial demands on several departments of the press. Damaris Kirchhofer, the editor responsible for the book, has been an enthusiastic supporter from the beginning. Her contributions and those of Don Yoder, working on a book of mine for the second time, have improved the style and presentation.

The references which accompany the text indicate the range of materials utilized in this examination of the cultural geography of Chinese rural housing. Aside from the tantalizing excursions into the topic by Liu Dunzhen in his 1957 book, very little appeared in Chinese publications for almost twenty-five years. It now is being revealed that substantial field work was carried out in the late 1950s and early 1960s to document vernacular housing as well as the more magnificent dwellings of gentry and merchants. Although very little was published then, much of these materials is now being reworked for publication. Aware of the pace of change in the countryside in recent years, many in China today are concerned that all too much of the past is being destroyed in the frenzied race toward modernization. Increasingly, Chinese architects and others are expressing the conviction that it is important not only that new dwellings and other buildings evoke the rich inherited tradition of China but that existing architectural forms of cultural and historical significance be preserved. It is being recognized that it is not only buildings of monumental significance which are worth examining and preserving but vernacular forms as well. The continuing preservation and documentation of this complex and vital patrimony will be an important dimension in defining the nature of China's future landscapes.

A NOTE ON CHINESE NAMES

CHINESE technical, place, and personal names are given using the *pinyin* system of romanization. Where a cited author has published in Chinese and English and uses in English a romanization form which differs from *pinyin,* this is indicated also in the references.

Introduction

THE Chinese countryside is legibly inscribed with patterns that reveal the purposeful efforts of peasants at meeting fundamental human needs. The agricultural environment has imposed upon China landscapes that have sustained a growing population over four millennia. Prominently placed among these fields are ubiquitous peasant houses, commonplace and simple structures that reflect generally the economy of scarcity characteristic of rural China. Ordinary houses are less remarkable for their antiquity than for the continuity of their form. Rising out of frugality rather than riches, vernacular forms, despite their nondescript appearance, nonetheless document a tradition in which experience and practical wisdom predominate.

Scholars have long concerned themselves with the architectural principles and symbolism of Chinese monumental buildings, such as temples, gentry mansions, palaces, walled cities, and imperial grave sites. They have concluded that the weight of precedent so characterizes the conservative building tradition of Chinese monumental architecture that forms and shapes discernible in prehistory and later in the earliest imperial capitals have been transmitted to recent times. Such classic architectural patterns are composed of conventionalized elements based upon well-defined concepts to the degree that a "Chinese building has a refreshing directness and functional clarity. . . . The greatest palace hall has a look of being a glorified farm building, and between the painted pavilion on the marble terrace and the humblest thatched hut there was real harmony" (Boyd 1962, 48).

Vernacular buildings were no doubt somewhat quieter in their formation than were the products of the grand tradition. They whisper, however, of the folk tradition, a composite idiom that reveals itself in the vernacular dwelling, which "bears perpetual witness to the slow pace of civilizations, of cultures bent on preserving, maintaining and repeating" (Braudel 1979, 267). A good deal of Chinese architecture is mere building, the enclosure of space, yet is still guided by cosmological sentiments and patterns of social relationships. At its most elegant, Chinese architecture is a sculptured expression of the cosmos.

Chapter 1 reviews the evolution of the Chinese dwelling from early times to the Ming dynasty. Drawing on archaeological and textual sources, the chapter explores prototypical house forms and their relationship to those which came later. A remarkable continuity of form, layout, and building materials is characteristic of Chinese dwellings. Changes over the years generally have been incremental rather than radical. References are made in the chapter to the linkages which tie anonymous buildings to those constructed for ceremonial and other less plebeian purposes.

During the sweep of Chinese history, continuing migration into diverse natural environments has shaped a variety of distinct cultural landscapes and forged China into a geographic entity characterized by cultural complexity. This territorial expansion, owing as much to the movement of peasants, refugees, traders, and entrepreneurs as it had to political and military actions, led to encounters with indigenous peoples of varying social and economic power. Acutely conscious of the natural environment, Chinese peasants built a variety of dwelling types, as presented in Chapter 2, that help to differentiate the diverse cultural milieux found within the country.

Rural houses by and large have been *built* rather than designed, with tradition acting as the regulator. Experience, practicality, and economy have guided housing form just as local conditions have governed building materials. Chapter 3 considers the common structural components of the Chinese rural house, stressing building materials and means of construction. Chinese houses generally have been built with impermanent materials such as pounded earth, wood, thatch, and bamboo with no conspicuous qualitative change in building materials until very recent times. Because Chinese builders usually separate those elements which support the roof from those which provide enclosure, the common framing systems and walling are discussed in detail.

The island of Taiwan, a frontier area for Chinese settlement, is used as a case study for treating the development of the house under changing sociocultural conditions. On Taiwan, migrants from the southeastern coastal provinces fashioned tributary communities that came to resemble in many ways their cultural hearths on the mainland. Chapter 4 highlights the relationship between the house and its occupants on Taiwan, where under evolving social circumstances, as well as new environmental options, the house took various forms. On Taiwan the structure and layout of the dwelling, as this chapter indicates, can be seen as humanized space and symbolic of family unity and aspirations. In its most mature form, the geometry of traditional Chinese dwellings underscores the concept of hierarchy in human relations.

Less tangible than the concrete and practical forms of the house itself, the Chinese folk tradition is nonetheless communicated in the layout and building of a traditional house. Chapter 5 reveals that houses, like graves, often have been sited with an attempt to comprehend cosmic patterns through the practice of the esoteric system known as *fengshui*. Chinese builders further have used almanacs, instruments, and charms in their pursuit of individualizing and optimizing the benefits of house construction.

The final chapter examines rural housing in contemporary China. After decades of neglect and decay, a veritable building boom by peasants has been occurring since 1979. Some of this work has been renovation and rehabilitation, but much more has been new construction. Carried out using traditional methods and forms, new house construction has created in rural China living environments which are often superior to those found in the crowded cities and which recognize that the dwelling is not simply a place of residence but is also often a center of production. Efforts at several levels are being made to adapt new materials and forms to meet the needs of rural construction. Yet despite such technical improvements, there is a remarkable continuity in rural house form. Where new rural housing is imitative of traditional patterns, it nonetheless reflects the changing contemporary social conditions in the country, such as the general trend toward reduction in family size.

Satisfying utilitarian needs in sheltering peasants from the vagaries of precipitation, temperature, and the wind, Chinese houses give meaning to the dynamic relationship binding people and environment. Yet, in giving shape to space, Chinese builders have produced more than basic structures. In molding materials and composing elements, they have been able to communicate, sometimes consciously and sometimes not, aspects of the vital folk tradition. As artifacts, Chinese dwellings resonate other aspects of Chinese society, echoing sociocultural elements linking the individual, family, and society and binding them all symbolically to the past. Fulfilling more than the need for shelter, dwellings indeed translate the Chinese ethos into physical form by creating basic units of social space.

The People's Republic of China

CHAPTER 1

The Historical Development of the Chinese House

FEW buildings of great antiquity exist today in China. This reflects the fact that the Chinese generally have not built in stone but have constructed their monuments and more common buildings of evanescent materials such as wood and earth. On the other hand, the *idea* of a building is of great age. It is preserved in classical texts, outlined in archaeological digs, and portrayed in paintings as well as in three dimensional clay models found in excavated tombs. Chinese buildings are basically nonchronological, less outstanding for their antiquity than for the continuity of form. Neither the city nor the countryside in China is a museum of progressively changing architectural styles. By and large, except for the architectural residuum of the western presence, one cannot readily see juxtaposed period pieces of bygone eras. The geographer Yi-fu Tuan (1969, 109) evokes the notion of an ahistorical landscape for China to describe this phenomenon, one in which the impression may be of age and permanence but instead the built environment tells only a limited "story."

No attempt has been made to elucidate fully the origin, development, and diffusion of Chinese domestic architecture. Evidence is substantial, however, that archetypal forms emerged early; these served as prototypes for successive developments that took form in different physical environments as migrants brought new areas within the Chinese pale. A refined treatment of the process of diffusion and a chronicle of derivative patterns must await further research (Tao 1984). Yet tantalizing glimpses of early forms and techniques of construction, as well as incipient cosmological underpinnings, are revealed even in a less than comprehensive examination of pedigreed as well as nonpedigreed buildings.

NEOLITHIC DWELLINGS

At the root of Chinese domestic architecture were the built forms of neolithic times found in the loessial areas of the middle reaches of the Huanghe (Yellow River) and in the marshy and wooded lower reaches of the Changjiang (Yangzi River). Arising in quite different physical environments, two distinct antecedents of later architectural patterns emerged. The character of these different forerunners and their neolithic cultural contexts have been revealed as the result of excavations in recent decades. As archaeological work continues in China, especially in the areas to the south of the

Qinling range, it is likely that a more complex and interrelated picture will develop. In the interim, some Chinese architectural historians and archaeologists present a fairly simple bimodal derivation—the cave and the nest—for later developments in domestic architecture.

Caves and nests (*xue* and *chao*), fashioned by neolithic settlers after unaltered natural models, have been noted by archaeologist Yang Hongxun (1980b) as the rudimentary antecedent forms of later Chinese derivative buildings. Figure 1.1 is a hypothetical sequence for the development of the *xue* from a horizontal lair through a vertical pocket pit to a semisubterranean covered pit and finally to a single room completely above the ground. This hypothetical progression would have been characteristic of north China. The horizontal and vertical pockets in the loessial soil served as proto-

types for the cave dwellings found even today in abundance in the same region. Hardly a product of architecture, these early dwellings lacked any formal roof; protection from the elements was secured by laying branches, leaves, and bark across the orifice when necessary. The pits, serving as embryonic forms in the proto-Chinese quest for shelter, provided insulation from the cold in winter as well as protection from the wind and rain (Liu Dunzhen 1957, 11–12).

The post-and-beam (*tailiang*) structural system depicted in the final part of the sequence in Figure 1.1 is the precursor of the basic Chinese framing system. In contrast, the *chao* seen in Figure 1.2 began as a roofed platform held within a single tree and evolved to a freestanding building on pillars by way of a sequence which brought the built form out of the tree. It is nonetheless supported

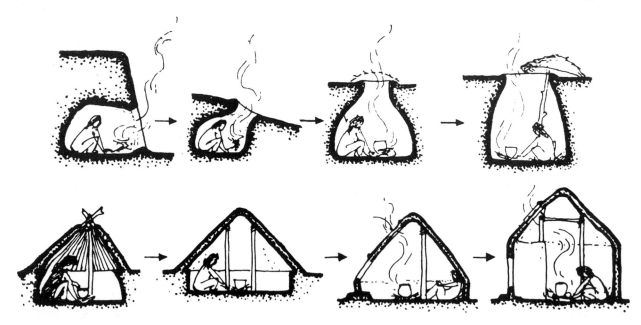

Figure 1.1. Hypothetical development of early dwellings in northern China. From top left to bottom right, the sequence evolves from a natural horizontal cave, a vertical pocketlike den with a fabricated roof, various semisubterranean pit dwellings with posts to support the roofs, and finally to surface dwellings with post-and-beam construction, culminating in a room defined by its walls.

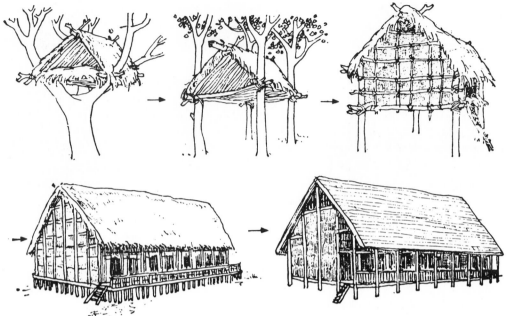

Figure 1.2. Hypothetical sequential development of early dwellings in the lower Yangzi area from a tree hut *(chao)* to dwellings utilizing posts and beams on the ground.

above the ground on treelike poles. The column and transverse tie *(chuandou)* system found in the mature form is viewed by Yang as the origin of this standard Chinese building technique. Both the *tailiang* and *chuandou* framing systems are discussed in detail in Chapter 3.

The neolithic site at Banpo, near today's northwestern city of Xian on the Wei River tributary of the Huanghe, presents more than the rudimentary outlines of successive building forms and concepts. Discovered in 1953 and excavated during the following four years, Banpo is representative of Yangshao culture of approximately 6000 B.C. (*Banpo yizhi* 1982, 1). Covering some 50,000 square meters, the nucleated village contained at least forty-five dwellings as well as animal pens, storage bins, kilns, and numerous graves. Excavations revealed two stages of occupancy. The first was characterized by circular, elliptical, and rectangular dwellings (Figure 1.3) built up from a

Figure 1.3. Reconstruction of a semisubterranean dwelling at Banpo neolithic site.

hollowed-out portion of the earth forming semisubterranean pits *(banxueju)*. Those of the later stage were larger, sometimes oblong in shape, and built of wooden frames directly on the ground. Stone tools, including axes, adzes, chisels, knives,

Figure 1.4. Reconstruction of circular neolithic houses. A separate roof is supported by pillars in the house in the foreground while the dwelling behind has walls bent to form a roof.

Figure 1.5. With overhanging eaves, a southern exposure, and windowless side and back walls, this neolithic rectangular dwelling at Banpo prefigured the later ubiquitous rural house style of north China.

and spades, were used to fashion building materials and to hollow out the subterranean base.

Among the semipit square dwellings, some reached 40 square meters in size although the average was closer to 20. The semipit was dug to a depth of 50 to 80 centimeters. Later circular and rectangular houses, as shown in Figures 1.4 and 1.5, were more likely built directly on the pounded earth. Wooden pillars, sunk into the soft windblown loessial soil, supported reed and mud plaster roofs with broad eaves of either conical or pyramidal shape. Walls were fashioned from wattle and daub. A striking characteristic of each dwelling was that the door faced south, an orientation that eventually achieved canonical sanction.

Archaeological evidence reveals that the neolithic villages of the middle reaches of the Huanghe existed in a physical environment quite different from that encountered today. Except for the loessial highlands which were semiarid, the hill slopes and lowlands near watercourses were at least subhumid and wooded. In the lower areas,

high water tables facilitated the digging of wells. Wood and reeds were abundant as was the ubiquitous loess, not only a construction medium easy to manipulate but a soil type conducive to agriculture because of its homogeneous texture, porosity, and friability (Figure 1.6). Scholars still disagree on the paleoecology of this region and the degree to which it differs from the situation today with limited rainfall and little natural plant life (Liu Dunzhen 1980, 23–27; Ho 1975, 21–35).

Farming, based on the staple millet, was facilitated by the easily worked loess. Domesticated animals and fishing provided subsidiary support. Yangshao neolithic culture as represented at Banpo is outstanding for the geometrically decorated pottery found at the site as well as the insights into early religious ideas suggested by patterns of burial. Numerous other contemporaneous and later neolithic sites have been excavated in the middle and lower sections of the Huanghe that confirm a commonality among neolithic dwellings in the region.

Separate neolithic developments in the lower

Figure 1.6. Deteriorating within ten years, some of the reconstructed dwellings at Banpo reveal their method of construction. Thin tree trunks are utilized to form the wall and roof supports to which grain stalks and reeds are affixed and plastered with a mixture of loessial mud and lime.

and middle reaches of the Changjiang (Yangzi River) have been discovered. Both circular and square-shaped shedlike dwellings apparently were built of saplings or stalks and mud placed upon a wooden structure. Where the water table was quite high and the terrain low-lying, dwellings were raised on stilts as a protection against moisture. Wooden pilings, bamboo rods, and branches were used in the construction of the

walls and roofs of dwellings at the Hemudu site, Yuyao county, Zhejiang province, dating from 7000 B.C. and discovered only in 1973. There is evidence even from incomplete excavations that these dwellings on stilts used mortise and tenon in their construction. Owing to the abundance of incendiary materials in the dwelling's structure, the stove was placed outside the lodging (Yang 1980a; Liu Dunzhen 1980, 27–28). A significant finding was the remains of cultivated rice, the earliest so far discovered in China. Bone plowshares and wooden plows are evidence of a well-developed agricultural system quite unlike that at Banpo.

XIA AND SHANG PERIODS

Traditional sources mark Chinese history as beginning with the Xia dynasty, which ran from the twenty-first to the sixteenth century B.C. Archaeological evidence on this period remains elusive, and there is no concrete indication of the types of dwellings that existed. Specialists such as Kwang-chih Chang (1976, 34–35) believe that there was a developmental continuation through the period which included semisubterranean houses and lime-plastered floors as well as tamped earth construction as elements.

Written history, however, begins only with the Shang dynasty, the successor to the Xia. Lasting more than six hundred years, the Shang was followed by the Zhou in 1122 B.C. During the Xia and Shang, viewed as slave-owning societies by contemporary Chinese historians, Chinese architectural patterns matured. The warm and well-watered conditions of the north China plain were strikingly different from conditions today. In this environment, a durable social, political, and religious system emerged which produced significant buildings.

A striking characteristic of the Shang period, differing from those of earlier times, was that settlements became more differentiated. While neolithic villages were largely self-contained, those of the Shang were constellations of residential units tied to administrative and service centers. This arrangement reflected the pyramidal society of the Shang: the king and royal lineages at the top, a middle stratum of civil and military officials, and a broad base of peasants. In the centers of administration and ceremony, imposing large buildings were raised upon tamped earth (*hangtu*) platforms with ample pillars supporting pitched roofs. Excavated sites reveal rectangular platforms that represent "a choice made consciously and consistently throughout the period" involving accurate measurements (Thorp 1983, 31). Beyond the center were satellite peasant settlements in which neolithic traditions continued. Here semisubterranean pits, sometimes plastered, with wooden supports as well as wattle and daub walls and roofing, marked no significant progression in common dwellings (Chang 1980, 78, 90–95, 340). It is significant that a majority of the larger square and rectangular buildings were oriented toward the south, although there was some variety. One scholar summarized developments by saying "it is scarcely an exaggeration to equate nobility with *hangtu*, and commonality with pit dwellings" (Wheatley 1971, 63). Convergence was still some time off.

Oracle bone inscriptions of the Shang period offer tantalizing indications of the shapes of diverse building types and architectural forms. Figure 1.7 shows characters in both their oracle bone forms and contemporary forms. They reveal pitched gabled roofs without an overhang and ridgepoles as characteristic of houses. In the case of palaces, a raised platform and overhanging eaves are indicated. The use of rammed earth

Figure 1.7. The representation of architectural characteristics in oracle bone inscriptions. The top row indicates characters referring to dwellings. Note the lack of eaves overhang and podium which are found associated with the characters for more prominent buildings in the second row.

foundations and walls as well as wood framing stand out to the degree that the Chinese have come to use the joined characters *tumu* (earth and wood) to signify architecture itself.

ZHOU, CHUNCHIU, AND ZHANGUO PERIODS

By the middle of the twelfth century B.C., a dependency of the Shang brought down the ruling house and established the Zhou, another clan-based dynastic sequence. During the following six hundred years, marked by a watershed in 770 B.C., the Zhou instituted far-reaching changes in society, thought, and politics. Sometimes termed the golden age of Chinese history, the Zhou was a vital period when viewed from a social and intellectual point of view. Great thinkers such as Confucius, Lao Zi, and Mo Zi elaborated social concepts that were to become normative for subsequent periods. The Chunchiu (Spring and Autumn) period from 722 to 421 B.C. was one of consolidation and expansion. It was followed by the Zhanguo (Warring States) period, which lasted until China's unification in 221 B.C.

At its greatest extent, Zhou territory reached

south of the Changjiang (Yangzi River), northeast into southern Manchuria, east to the Shandong peninsula, and west into Gansu. This area far exceeded the domain dominated by the Shang. Thus the variety of natural environments offered more diverse and greater challenges than those of earlier times. Extensive urbanization was supported by an increasingly prosperous agricultural sector. All land was nominally owned by the Zhou royal house and hereditary fiefdoms were granted to nobles. These in turn controlled rural populations described today by mainland historians as slaves but given a less ideological interpretation by western historians. Peasants lived in rudimentary houses in settlements called *yi* and *she*.

The architectural characteristics of this lengthy transitional era are known from excavations and texts. Significant areal expansion of urban sites was accompanied by an evolutionary path which transformed administrative/ceremonial centers by adding important commercial functions. Yet "commercial activities . . . were but poorly developed by any absolute standard, and the vast majority of city dwellers . . . were cultivators who, in summer at any rate, went out daily through the city gates to work in their fields" (Wheatley 1971, 178).

It is the morphology and construction of the Zhou city which draws the attention of the architect. Patterns revealed here in urban form, however, replicate themselves later in the domestic architecture of rural areas as well. Anticipating the courtyard style *(siheyuan)* of later urban domestic architecture, the dwellings of nobles centered about an axis running north and south and included an entrance gate as well as a facing hall. Structures had parallel symmetry. A large residence excavated at Zhaochencun in Shaanxi province contained a foundation and interior walls made of pounded earth. Rising above this

foundation was a wooden framework which carried the weight of a tiled roof. At the top of each pillar sat a *dou*, or elongated block, to reduce the span and, by increasing the surface contact, carry the weight of the beams and roof above. Joined with a *gong* or supporting bow-shaped arm to form a *dougong* bracket set, these forms served as the precursors of those which reached their apex during the Song and Tang periods as distinctive and indispensable elements of palaces and many larger residences. Originating as a structural member, the *dougong* subsequently evolved often into a purely decorative element.

So intimate was the association of the Zhou city with the wall which confined it that the same character *cheng* was used to denote both. The Zhou city wall was itself considered a "building," constructed of pounded earth or *hangtu*. Among the oldest methods of making walls, including those for dwellings and enclosing courtyards, tamped earth construction is still used widely in the northern provinces. Such walls were laboriously raised, usually during the autumn months, by beating down the soft loessial soil held between a mobile frame. Archaeologists have shown that the dimensions of Zhou walls ranged as much as 15 meters in both height and width, no doubt presenting impressive features on the broad landscapes of north China. Within the walls, important ceremonial and residential buildings were themselves set upon tamped earth platforms.

The cosmologically ideal shape of the Zhou city was the square, a form that sometimes was altered to a rectangle. It is not possible to say exactly why the Chinese opted for a four-sided figure but it no doubt invited cosmological sanction: the earth perceived as a square against a round heaven. Emblematic numbers appear as well, expressed in the prescription that each side of the wall should be 9 *li* (each *li* about one-third mile) in length, each side pierced by three gates with nine broad streets running within the city walls from north to south and east to west. This canonical form, aligned with cardinal orientation and axiality, foreshadowed the patterning of later imperial capitals and dwellings. Builders combined ritual symbolism with engineering exigency in the selection of lowland sites for walled cities. Geometrical space became a cosmo-magical symbol. Zhou cities were sited using divinatory measures, principles of geomancy, to ensure a propitious location. Cities generally faced south, the direction associated with the *yang*—the sun and life-giving forces. Reference was made to the celestial pole:

The Ting-star is in the middle of the sky;
We begin to build the palace at Ch'u.
Orienting them by the rays of the sun
We set to work on the houses at Ch'u,
By the side of them planting hazels and chestnut trees,
Catalpas, Pawlownias, lacquer trees
That we may make the zithers great and small.

[*Shijing,* trans. Waley 1937, 281]

A symbolism of the center with striking centripetality, massive gate structures of significant architectural prominence, as well as a schema of receding depth—these elements came to characterize not only the archetypal city but also full-form dwellings. The palace of the Zhou ruler was placed in the center, facing southward, and constituted a city within a city. As cosmic diagram, the Zhou city and its constituent buildings represented at a macroscale patterns that prefigure later developments even in common dwellings.

During Zhou times the common peasants no doubt lived as they had in Shang times, in semi-subterranean or surface dwellings with a cover built of tree limbs and wattle and daub. Increasingly with the removal of woodland because of agricultural expansion, it seems likely that many

builders dug into the loessial cliffs to form caves, a dwelling type that is still prominent in northwestern China. Pit dwellings were not built in the vicinity of the Changjiang (Yangzi River), but semipile dwellings were built in recognition of drainage problems in the low-lying areas. Roof tiles of various sorts made their appearance during the Zhou period and began to play an increasing role in solving problems of waterproofing of roofs. The diffusion of roof tiles during the Chunchiu period contributed to the flattening of the slope of roofs from the 1:3 common with thatched roofs to 1:4 with tiled roofs. Semicircular eaves tiles *(wadang),* some decorated and others plain, increasingly became fashionable among the wealthy (Liu Dunzhen 1980, 38–39). As evidenced on bronze vessels created at the end of this period, technical achievements in the use of wood led to some buildings reaching two or three stories; brackets *(dougong)* were being used extensively to support the beams and the weight of the roof (Liu Dunzhen 1957, 17).

THE QIN TRANSITION

The later centuries of the Zhou period centered on the Warring States era, a crucible of history from which China emerged unified in 221 B.C. by the victorious Qin emperor. Although this first imperial dynasty was short-lived and left no significant mark on domestic architecture, it bequeathed to posterity the magnificent terra-cotta warriors and horses of Xian, the unopened tomb of the Qin emperor Shihuang, the standardization of weights and measures, and portions of the Great Wall. Fundamentally, this brief dynasty served as the threshold of the Han dynasty, which lasted from 202 B.C. to A.D. 220. During this period, new standards of technological achievement were reached.

Progress During the Han Dynasty

The Han dynasty, divided into a western period centered on Changan (today's Xian) and a later eastern period focused on Luoyang, was a period of extensive territorial expansion involving military conquest and colonization. Migration brought the evolving architectural tradition into contact with local non-Chinese patterns and lead to a mosaic of architectural forms. Depictions of house forms in drawings and in low relief on tiles as well as actual models taken from period tombs reveal the precise nature of the house of the time. By virtue of their existence, these dwellings generally represent what may be termed "country houses" rather than those of the rural masses (Boyd 1962, 87).

Funerary objects *(mingqi)* of the Han period taken from graves throughout China reveal house forms of various types. Although single-storied dwellings *(pingfang)* existed, most of the funerary models of houses are of two stories. The upper story served as living quarters and was connected to the courtyard below by a ladderlike stair. The ground floor courtyard was used for livestock. Some dwellings were made of brick even though brick was expensive in most areas. The tiled roofs generally lacked pronounced curvature, although the ridge line in some cases sweeps upward at each end. Carried into this period also was the neolithic practice of a composition roof of a mud mixture and stalks rather than tile.

Figure 1.8 shows several pottery models of dwellings of the Han period discovered in graves in Guangdong province in southern China. These include the shape of a carpenter's square *(quchi)* with two segments joined at right angles embracing a small courtyard and a two story U-shaped dwelling with a prototypical front courtyard *(san-*

heyuan). A somewhat larger and more complex dwelling, shown in Figure 1.9, is represented by an engraving found on a Han brick in Sichuan province. The enclosure is surrounded by a wall that is topped with a tile roof. Divided into two, the left-hand division is the more important with the living quarters and two courtyards. The prin-

Figure 1.8. L-shaped and U-shaped dwellings as represented in funerary models from the Han dynasty.

Figure 1.9. An engraved brick representing a large dwelling in Sichuan province during the Han dynasty.

cipal building, framed in wood and capped with tile, is composed of three bays and is axially placed on a podium facing the major courtyard. Although, as in earlier times, the figures sit on the floor, beds and cots for kneeling began to appear during this period. The right-hand division is separated from the residential compound by a wall and a gate. It is clearly subsidiary, confining within it a well, kitchen, and area for drying clothing. Prominent is a multistoried timber-framed tower used for surveillance as well as secure storage of valuables. Rather than the gabled roof of the dwelling, this watchtower has a widely overhanging hipped roof supported by bracket sets, or *dougong* (Liu Dunzhen 1984, 52–53).

Still other discoveries, such as those in Shandong since 1953, reveal the full flowering of the symmetrical courtyard pattern. These patterns were further developed in the residences of the nobility as seen in numerous stone reliefs found in

Han tombs. The progression from simple, axially oriented longitudinal shapes through multistoried L-shaped forms to the regularized courtyard pattern reveals increasing conformity to societal norms and accompanied increases in wealth and status. Larger residences mirrored the layout of temples and palaces, which themselves usually were encircled by walls and characterized by a sequence of courtyards that revealed both space and the overall configuration only gradually to the pedestrian.

HOUSING BETWEEN THE HAN AND SUI

The three hundred years between the downfall of the Han dynasty and the establishment of the Sui dynasty in 581 was a period of political division, warfare, barbarian invasion, and a general withering of the economy. Domestic architecture is represented in only a minor way in the archaeological and artistic legacy of the period. The most significant architectural features of China during this period rose out of the expansion and absorption of Buddhism. By the fourth century, a sinicized Buddhist faith was spreading among the gentry. Buddhism flowered with the patronage of Emperor Wu in the early years of the fifth century. Some gave their large residences as acts of charity to become transformed into Buddhist temples, setting a pattern in which little difference came to distinguish secular and religious buildings. Others vied in granting land and funds for the construction of monasteries and temples. The most notable architectural legacy of this period was the building of magnificent cave temples and pagodas, important not only for their artistic significance but for their engineering achievement as well.

The degree to which Buddhism affected the houses of the masses at this time cannot be determined, although in later periods even folk dwellings came to be nourished by Buddhist traditions. Fu Xinian (1984, 24), an eminent contemporary architectural historian, sees new syntheses taking place during this interval of division: "Architectural styles also gradually shed the archaic simplicity and solidness of the Western and Eastern Han, evolving into expansiveness and fullness and setting the precondition for attaining the next high peak of the following stage in the Sui and Tang period."

SUI AND TANG DEVELOPMENTS

Large-scale engineering works were carried out during the short-lived Sui dynasty using the conscripted labor of millions of Chinese. Among these monumental tasks were the fortification of the Great Wall, the construction of two capitals at an impressive scale, and major canal building, including the Grand Canal linking the surplus water areas of the lower Yangzi and the deficient areas of the middle and lower Huanghe. Like the Qin dynasty, which presaged the imperial Han period, the Sui fell in a few decades as a result of peasant uprisings, thus heralding the arrival of a golden age under the Tang from 618 to 906.

Except for representations in paintings, no examples of domestic architecture exist from the Sui period. Figures 1.10 and 1.11 show two simple dwellings that were portrayed in a scroll painted during the Sui dynasty by Zhan Ziqian. Both enclose a courtyard, but the *siheyuan* courtyard style is distinquished from the *sanheyuan* by the placement of a building at the entrance where the *sanheyuan* simply has a gate. Except for the thatched roof on one wing of the *sanheyuan,* all the roofs are of tile with simple gables. Both these examples clearly express axiality as well as proportional symmetry and provide a configuration

emblematic of mature Chinese domestic architecture. Such dwellings are today still common in south central China. The configuration of Sui dwellings continued into the Tang period, but the rationale for the use of space differed significantly in the two dynasties. In the case of Sui rural dwellings, the courtyard layout effectively embraced utilitarian space needed by the peasants while those outlined in later Tang houses usually served more frivolous and purely symbolic functions (Liu Dunzhen 1957, 20). As in Han times, a thousand years earlier, two-story buildings were common.

Muyao, or wooden magic, has been used to describe the palatial residences of officials during the Tang dynasty. Set among landscapes of prosperity, some country villas *(bieye)* included multiple courtyards framed by extravagantly furnished buildings that held luxurious bric-a-brac brought from afar. They were sometimes accompanied by gardens which included mock mountains and pools. One mentioned in a poem by Bai Juyi encompassed an area of 17 *mu* (approximately 1.1 hectares) with one-third of the area given over to the dwelling, one-fifth given over to water, and one-ninth planted in bamboo (Liu Dunzhen 1984, 125). Extant Tang buildings include four wooden Buddhist temples and several masonry pagodas that only hint at the grandeur of the times. No residences, imperial buildings, or wooden pagodas survive from the Sui and Tang. Those few buildings that remain portray the significant use of modular systems of construction and the fact that wood frame construction had fully matured by the tenth century.

SONG ARCHITECTURAL PATTERNS

The period from the disintegration of the Tang dynasty in 906 to the rise of the Northern Song in

Figure 1.10. With rooms at the front forming a *siheyuan* courtyard, a fully developed configuration characterizes this dwelling as part of a landscape painted during the Sui period by Zhan Ziqian in a scroll "Travelling at Springtime."

Figure 1.11. Somewhat similar to the *siheyuan,* this *sanheyuan,* which appears in the same scroll as the previous figure, simply has a gate structure framing the courtyard. The dwelling itself, while preserving axiality and symmetry, is constructed of simpler materials that include bamboo and thatch. Its overall form is quite compact.

960 was an interlude of disunity, but one in which there were no sharp breaks in the evolution of Chinese social, cultural, economic, and political patterns. Much briefer than the four centuries between the fall of the Han and the rise of the Sui and Tang, this interlude was but a transient stage in the further maturation of architectural forms. For a century and a half, the Northern Song from its capital at Kaifeng along the Huanghe brought about a comprehensive economic and social transformation. A highly productive agricultural base emerged as a result of significant technological innovations, the expansion of arable land, population growth which reached 100 million, and the mass penetration of the population into the south.

This development was further encouraged by the movement of the Song capital to Hangzhou in the lower Changjiang (Yangzi River) area in 1127 as a result of the displacement of the Song ruling house from the north by a victorious tribe whose origins were in Manchuria. By the thirteenth century, more than eighty percent of the country's population was in the south as compared to forty to forty-five percent in the eighth century. The reclamation of land, the spread of water control, the popularization of agricultural manuals, and transportation improvements all contributed to the accumulation of wealth among those living in rural areas. Animated by these factors, it is likely that improvements in basic shelter for the peasant population came about as well.

No dwellings remain from the six hundred years that spanned the period from the Tang through the Song, yet characteristics of the architecture of the times can be gleaned from a Song manual and extant religious buildings which express the direction of architectural development. Li Jie, an imperial building supervisor, completed in 1100 a manual for palace-style buildings titled *Yingzao fashi* (Building Standards). One of its

purposes was to codify the principles underlying the construction of wood frame structures. Such buildings were not consciously "designed" in the architectural sense to express any artistic style. Rather, they were crafted by carpenters who were knowledgeable of the intrinsic qualities of timber and the accumulated experience of earlier craftsmen. *Yingzao fashi* set down standardized rules relating to the use of lumber, mud, tile, bamboo, and paint. It included detailed descriptions of jointing and brick manufacture as well as calculations relating to the amount of labor required to complete tasks. Detailed drawings, generally presented from the craftsman's perspective, fleshed out the standardization efforts (Liang 1983; Glahn 1981, 162ff; 1984, 48ff).

Special attention was given to the bracket sets *(dougong)* in this manual since the bracket arm was taken as the fundamental dimension. According to the manual, "all rules for constructing houses have the standard dimension as their base. . . . The height and depth of eaves of each house, the size of each nameable structural member, the force of the bent and the straightness of each curve of the roof, accordance with the measuring instruments of the carpenter: the pair of compasses, the square, the plumb line and the ink string, in every case the units of standard dimension constitute the rule" (*Yingzao fashi,* after Glahn 1982, 27–28). Sumptuary regulations further defined the nature of housing for the different social classes of the time. In codifying and differentiating such fundamental aspects of life as shelter, the Song manual presented a collection of paradigms that guided the construction and decoration of dwellings for centuries to come.

Song architecture was no doubt influenced by the experiences gained as the south was consolidated, resulting in the blending of a tradition with roots in the soft loessial soils of the drier north with that of the well-watered lower reaches of the Changjiang. Intricate workmanship, accentuated with polychrome designs, came to characterize palaces and temples, as well as large residences, as can be seen (Figure 1.12) in Song paintings (Liu Dunzhen 1957, 21).

THE MONGOL INTERLUDE

A century of alien Mongol rule, beginning in 1260 and lasting to 1368, brought a degree of political unity to East Asia that had not existed since the decline of the Tang dynasty in 907. Although built for the Mongol emperor, the capital at Dadu (on the site of present-day Beijing) was guided by traditional Chinese norms for lay-

ing out a capital and palaces within. Neither palaces nor residences remain from the Mongol rule under the dynastic name of Yuan. The few extant religious buildings suggest to one architectural historian that Yuan architecture "was more sparing in the use of material, exhibiting slenderer columns and smaller *dougong,* and tending toward a softer and gentler style, which was less soaring and powerful than that of Tang and Song architecture" (Fu 1984, 30).

The evidence does not permit any definitive statement concerning the dwellings of Chinese peasants, however. Certain policies of the Mongols no doubt insulated the Han peasantry from the influence of the Mongols and others. A rigid distinction separated the Mongols from both *Han-*

Figure 1.12. Rural dwelling with roofs of thatch and tile as depicted in the Song painting *Qingming shanghe tu.*

ren, Chinese in the north, and *manzu,* an abusive term used to describe the Chinese and others living in the south. Although efforts made to foster agricultural growth and extend domestic trade must have benefited some peasants and led to the expansion and improvement of rural dwellings, there does not appear to have been any innovation in rural dwellings during this time.

MING DWELLINGS

The earliest dwellings extant in China are from the Ming period (1368–1644) with larger numbers from the Qing (1644–1912). None of these are the residences of common peasants but for the most part are those of merchants and gentry even when they are found in rural areas. Like palace and temple buildings, the fully developed dwellings of those with wealth and status include a repertoire of common elements that nonetheless are shared with more modest peasant houses. Comprehensive sumptuary regulations guided the scale and decorative embellishment of dwellings as signals of the owner's rank and status through-

out most of this period. Peasants, even as they acquired wealth, were thus generally restrained from constructing large dwellings except sometimes in areas remote from imperial authority. Commoners from the Tang dynasty onward were legally permitted only to have houses that did not exceed three bays.

Somewhat modest two-story dwellings that date to the Ming period have been discovered in Huizhou in the southeastern section of Anhui province. Found in compact villages and towns or set individually among the fields, they took various forms as shown in Figure 1.13. The gable profiles are similar to those shown later as the *yingshanding* ("firm mountain roof") types in Figure 3.46 and Plate 7. Built compactly of brick, they generally did not exceed three bays in width and included only a small skywell *(tianjing)* rather than a substantial interior courtyard. Exterior walls were whitewashed and without decoration while elaborately carved wood characterized the ceilings, roof members, balustrades, and upper windows within. In each of these dwellings a main hall serving ceremonial purposes was set at the

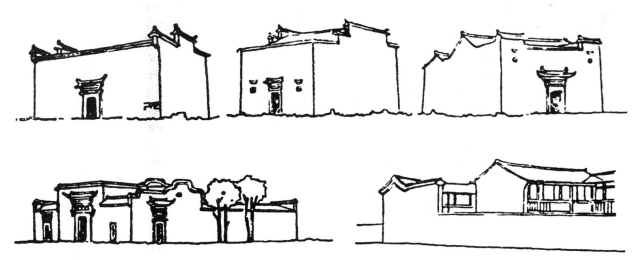

Figure 1.13. Exterior views of Ming dynasty houses in Huizhou, Anhui province.

center of the rear section. Flanked by living space, the main hall centralized the ancestral paraphernalia of the occupants. Bedrooms typically were placed on the better-ventilated second floor (Zhang et al. 1957; Cheng and Hu 1980; Boyd 1962, 92–103; Shan 1984). Dwellings and other architectural forms of the Ming period have been discovered in recent years in other areas of the country as well, including Jingdezhen in Jiangxi, Tongtingdongshan in Jiangsu, and Dingcun in Shanxi. Except for brief mention, none has been described in detail (Jingdezhen 1981, 42).

SUMMARY

A remarkable continuity of form and layout is characteristic of Chinese dwellings from earliest times through the late imperial period. No conspicuous innovations in material and technique interrupted the evolutionary process, and no striking differences emerged to differentiate monumental and more plebeian buildings. For both types of structures, earth and wood rather than stone were the principal building materials even when alternatives were readily available. Size and proportion were influenced by convention and sumptuary regulations, establishing scale and the refinement of decoration as the principal means of differentiation. Flexibility, guided by a sense of precedence related to patterns of human relationships, generally ordered the utilization of interior space. Chinese houses were less designed than built and emphasized convention rather than novelty.

CHAPTER 2

The Variety of
Chinese Rural Dwellings

VERNACULAR dwellings represent the common-place and simple structures of the rural population. Many can be labeled as nondescript, plain, or even ugly. Although they hardly epitomize China's grand architectural traditions, the folk patterns of rural housing nonetheless echo these traditions. As the preceding chapter indicates, the archetypal antecedents of Chinese vernacular and monumental architectural forms appeared quite early and had reached a high stage of development by the Tang and Song periods. Except for tantalizing glimpses of domestic architecture gleaned from archaeological excavations and art, no dwellings remain in China from before the Ming dynasty (1368–1644). Nonetheless, common folk dwellings changed little in most locales in China until the present, confirming Fernand Braudel's assertion of the "strength of precedent." For the most part, one may look at a twentieth-century rural dwelling and see one of an earlier time. This chapter examines a selection of the distinct types of dwellings found in rural areas in the twentieth century and points to the common heritage which binds them to their ancestral forms.

SETTLEMENT AND HOUSING PATTERNS

Rural housing in China is found clustered in nucleated settlements or dispersed individually among the fields (Plates 1–9). Nucleated villages typically comprise a somewhat compact ensemble of dwellings surrounded by fields as seen in the hill lands of Zhejiang province (Figure 2.1). Characteristic walls and gates often screen the individual houses from passersby as in Figure 2.2, which shows the main lane passing through a nucleated village in southern Shaanxi province. Large nucleated villages that rival small towns in size are found on the plains of northern and northwestern China. Smaller nucleated villages are also found throughout the country such as the one shown in northeastern Hebei province in Figure 2.3. They are especially common in the hilly areas of southern China. Dispersed villages, as seen in Figures 2.4, 2.5, and 2.6, are made up of freestanding houses or small groupings of houses in hamlets situated among the fields. Dispersed villages, like nucleated villages, are bound as a

Figure 2.1. This nucleated village at the foot of Moganshan in western Zhejiang province is set beneath bamboo-forested hills and adjacent to rice fields.

Figure 2.2. This tree-lined lane of a compact village in southern Shaanxi province reveals only tamped earth walls and entry gates to the private courtyards and dwellings.

Figure 2.3. Small nucleated village in northern Hebei province. Facing south, each dwelling has a walled courtyard with a kitchen garden, grain storage bin, and latrine.

Figure 2.4. Individual dwellings collectively make up a dispersed village near Nanjing, Jiangsu province.

Figure 2.5. Set amid geometrically regular rice fields, this large residential compound is part of a dispersed village in Fujian province.

Figure 2.6. This farmstead is isolated atop a ridge on the outskirts of Guilin, Guangxi Zhuang Autonomous Region.

community by factors that go beyond mere proximity.

Common and distinctive elements characterize Chinese building plans ranging from humble dwellings to palaces and from preimperial times to the present. Exceptions and variations due to regional ethnic, historical, and environmental conditions have bequeathed a legacy of apparent diversity—still, however, insufficient to mask the common tradition. This diversity includes a multiplicity of basic patterns including not only rectangular shapes but also round and U-shaped designs, as well as unique large enclosures and cave dwellings (Spencer 1947; Liu Dunzhen 1957, 22–51).

Built largely of earth and wood, Chinese houses utilize local raw materials and draw on a building tradition that reaches to antiquity. Some dwellings possess characteristic features that link them visually to the architectural heritage of China's great palaces and temples. Most, however, reflect the fully developed architectural tradition only in a restrained fashion. Expressive of the multiethnic makeup of the country, some dwellings like that of the round yurt in Figure 2.7 are strictly regional forms and characteristic of non-Han ethnic minority traditions of pastoralism where ease of dismantling was a necessary precondition. Others like the multistoried circular ensembles found in Fujian and Guangdong provinces are peculiar to a Han ethnic subgroup, in this case the Kejia or Hakka. Cave dwellings, found in great numbers

Figure 2.7. Found in Inner Mongolia and Xinjiang autonomous regions, the wood-framed yurt is covered with layers of felt. This yurt is utilized by Kazakhs, a minority nationality, during their summer sojourn to the pastures of the Tianshan mountains, Xinjiang Uygur Autonomous Region.

in the loessial uplands in the middle reaches of the Huanghe (Yellow River), still are important forms of housing for millions of Chinese.

NORTHERN HOUSES

Whether found freestanding in dispersed settlements or clustered together in nucleated villages, the ubiquitous rectangular rural houses found throughout north China derive from the penury of the peasant population. As economic conditions allowed, small houses have been renovated and enlarged. The shape and organization of interior space show an early and continuing understanding of ways to overcome climatic problems. North China is largely a region of continental climate in which there is great disparity between summer and winter temperatures, with ranges usually exceeding 30 °C. Winter temperatures dip well below zero throughout most of the region and rise beyond 30 °C in the summer. Rainfall is generally below 500 millimeters and is concentrated mostly in the three months of summer. Dry winter winds together with spring dust storms pummel much of the region from the north and northwest for more than six months of each year. In such an environment, timber seldom has been abundant and peasants have looked to the soil for their building materials. Generally speaking, the soil on the north China plain is composed of alluvial silt brought to the region by deposition of the Huanghe, China's river of mud which acquired its silt load as the river eroded the fine windblown loess in its middle reaches.

The typical north China rural dwelling traditionally has been a one-story rectangle with a depth of only a single room. At its simplest, the dwelling is a small space enclosed by four walls lengthening into a substantial rectangle as circumstances permitted. Figures 2.8, 2.9, and 2.10 represent common types of multiple-bay dwellings. Reflecting the fact that the character for ridgepole (dong) is composed of elements for "east" and "wood," the ridgepole supporting the roof of most northern dwellings is arranged in an east-west direction. Accordingly, the facade is oriented so that the door and windows face south, canonical considerations typical of Chinese palaces that give evidence of a comprehensive and striking climatic adaptation. Typically no windows or doors break the other walls. The southern orientation of these simple plans creates satisfactory passive solar conditions.

Dwellings similar to these are found not only on the north China plain but in the surrounding hill lands as well. Variations, such as the rolled roof in Figure 2.11 and the high pitched roof in Figure 2.12, are found in the northeastern region of the country beyond the Great Wall. Where such common rectangular rural houses are found in compact villages or on hill slopes, their layout usually continues to maintain a south-facing axis with the courtyard forced to vary in shape and orientation.

Known colloquially as the "one open, two closed" type (yiming liangan), the typical dwelling of three bays (jian or kaijian) presents a layout of two bedrooms separated by a central room which serves as corridor and utility area (Figure 2.13). Just inside the door of the central common room is a low brick stove to each side, serving not only cooking needs but providing heat in winter for the dwelling (Figure 2.14). Traditionally, either an image of the Kitchen God or a written representation of his name was pasted above the stove. The central stove has important symbolic meaning in the household since it signifies family unity. If a family were to divide, even though they occupy the same dwelling, this arrangement commonly would be signaled by the placement of individual cooking facilities and Kitchen Gods for each of the

Figure 2.8. Single-sloped shedlike roof on a two-room dwelling, central Shanxi province. Note the fully exposed front. A plan and elevation of a similar dwelling are shown in Figure 3.33.

Figure 2.9. Double-sloped roof on a brick and stone dwelling near Datong, northern Shanxi. The house has a courtyard enclosed by a stone wall.

Figure 2.10. A multiple-bay dwelling typical of the north China plain, northern Hebei province.

Figure 2.11. Rolled sheet iron covers the roof of this dwelling in northeastern China. Note the plastered adobe walls.

Figure 2.12. High-pitched roof on a five-*jian* rectangular house in the southern part of northeastern China.

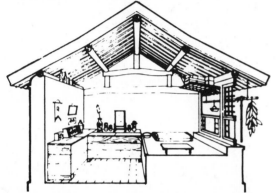

Figure 2.13. Interior views of a three-bay *(jian)* dwelling built in the traditional style found north of Beijing. The top longitudinal perspective is from the rear showing two bedrooms with a *kang* brick bed in each along the southern wall. Between these rooms is a common room with facing stoves flanking the entrance. The bottom figure showing the eastern bedroom reveals the structural components of the dwelling, including pillar-and-beam construction with curtain walls.

Figure 2.14. Flanking the entrance door to many north China rural houses are brick stoves that in winter not only serve for cooking purposes but also provide heat through flues to the *kang* beds in adjacent rooms.

smaller family units. In summer, a temporary cooking shed might be located outside in order to keep the house cool.

Dominating each of the adjacent bedrooms is a *kang,* an elevated bed platform made of earthen bricks which in winter becomes a heat-dissipating surface for the hot air which passes from the cooking stoves through a warren of flues embedded within each *kang.* Because the earthen bricks become impregnated with gases from the stove, peasants in the past found value in periodically dismantling their *kang,* breaking the bricks into powder, and mixing it with manure for use as a chemically rich fertilizer. Located just inside the south-facing windows, the *kang* act also as solar collectors for the winter sun. The warmest spot in a house during the coldest times of the year is the *kang.*

By custom, the eastern bedroom is given to the senior generation where it serves also as parlor and dining room. For much of the year the room is the center of family life. The elevated *kang,* even in summer, is a bright and surprisingly cool place for domestic chores such as sewing and food preparation (Plate 10). The more valuable articles belonging to the household are usually kept in this room since it is rarely unoccupied. The opposite bedroom is used by other members of the family, including a married son, his wife, and children. This room, like the kitchen, serves as the place to store grain and other food stocks, farm implements, and similar items that cannot be left outside. Clothing and bedding are stored in stacked trunks at the end of the *kang* since this area is likely to stay dry. Each room typically contains a bucket (wooden, pottery, or enameled) so that the family need not use the outside privy at night.

Traditional northern houses generally present a spartan appearance (Figure 2.15) broken only by the sometimes colorful decoration of their windows and doors as illustrated in Figure 2.8 and Plate 9. The front of the house often is untidy and site of a latrine, a well, storage space for wood and straw, as well as improvised pens for raising a few chickens, ducks, or a pig (Figure 2.16). Contemporary designers give a good deal of attention to improving the layout of the outside area since what it contains can affect the health of the household. In order to preserve the southern exposure, the expansion of the dwelling when possible takes place laterally through the addition of new bays as needed. In some areas, the new structures might be placed at right angles to the main building although an obvious shortcoming is the altered orientation away from the direct rays of the midday winter sun. The construction of high walls to join the buildings around an enclosed courtyard sometimes was needed for security and provided a buffer from the winter and spring winds.

Classifying a house as a northern type is an exercise in distilling common characteristics even when there are stylistic differences. There is no complete uniformity in the patterns and styles of houses found on the north China plain, in the surrounding hills, or in the northeast. There are, however, sufficient similarities in layout as well as

Figure 2.15. The plain appearance of this dwelling in Hebei province is in contrast to those shown in Figure 2.8 and Plate 9. The shallow eaves overhang provides space for drying corn.

Figure 2.16. Enclosed by a wall, the courtyard of this peasant dwelling in northern Hebei province includes storage space for wood and straw, grain silos, chicken coops and pigpens, a well, and a latrine.

methods and materials of construction to justify treating the great variety of housing in these regions as a single type.

LOESSIAL EARTH-SHELTERED DWELLINGS

Some 40 million Chinese live in earth-sheltered dwellings in the loessial uplands of northwestern China, principally in the provinces of Gansu, Shaanxi, Shanxi, and Henan. Archaeological findings give evidence of the patrimony of excavated subterranean dwellings that reaches back some seven thousand years. Considering the areal extent and continuing development of this some-

what unusual housing form, these cavelike dwellings should not be looked at simply as a backward and transitory form of shelter. In fact, in recent years two national conferences have been held to examine the nature and future of subterranean houses in northern China. Chinese peasants and housing designers both have been seeking ways to overcome deficiencies in existing dwellings and find means to build more satisfactory caves.

The ocher loessial uplands cover some 400,000 square kilometers, presenting a landscape dramatically etched by natural forces. In an area of limited rainfall, generally less than 400 millimeters, the natural environment is very dry and denuded, covered often only by a thick mantle of fine windblown silt carried into the region from the Mongolian uplands. The loess, *huangtu* or "yellow earth," blankets some areas of the region to a depth of 200 meters. Although it compacts well vertically, the soil nonetheless easily erodes into a dissected landscape especially under the impact of summer thunderstorms. Lacking wood and without the economic wherewithal to bring in building materials from the outside, peasants traditionally have dug into the soil to make houses which cost only a quarter of surface dwellings.

Two general types of loessial earth-sheltered dwellings can be seen throughout the region. Figures 2.17 and 2.18 depict cliffside caves *(kaoshan yaodong)* found in Shanxi province; Figure 2.19 is a perspective drawing of sunken courtyard caves

(aoting yaodong, diyao or *tianjingyuan yaodong)* in Henan province. These dwellings of various sizes consist of rooms excavated into the steeply dissected sides of loessial hills. Small cave dwellings generally do not exceed a depth of 10 meters, although larger caves may reach 20. In height they rarely stretch higher than 5 meters. Since the width is largely a function of the calcareous content of the soil, where the lime content is high there is greater coherency to the loess and a possibility of spanning distances to a maximum of 5 meters (Hou 1982, 72). Because damp soil is least desirable for caves, peasants try to choose a high location that is not too far from a well source. Any newly built cave takes upward of three months to dry out completely. A cave of approximately 19

Figure 2.17. Perspective view of *kaoshan yaodong* in the loessial uplands north of Lishi, Shanxi province.

Figure 2.18. *Kaoshan yaodong* north of Lishi, Shanxi province. Some of the caves have been faced with brick. A tamped earth wall forms a courtyard for many of them. The ventilating chimneys protrude above the caves.

chi (about 6 meters) deep, 10 *chi* (about 3 meters) high, and 9 *chi* (about 3 meters) wide takes about forty days to excavate and can be used for several generations as long as it is properly maintained (Myrdal 1965, 45).

Figures 2.20, 2.21, and 2.22 show the exterior and interior views of a cliffside dwelling located to the northwest of Xian in Shaanxi province. Providing a residence for seven people in three separate chambers, the cave complex includes two bedrooms located in adjacent but unconnected chambers, a deep cave for cooking and storage, and a large courtyard defined by a 3-meter-high tamped earth wall. This particular cave complex includes one frame bed and a common northern Chinese *kang*. The room with the *kang* maintains its location directly inside the window as in common northern houses, but the room with the frame bed observes the principle known as *qiantang houshi* (main room in front, bedroom in back). In this rectangular cave room, no partition separates the space for each use. The arcuate walls of each are papered with newspapers, colorful posters, and photographs. The courtyard is entered from the road via a path through a prominent gate in the southeastern corner of the tamped

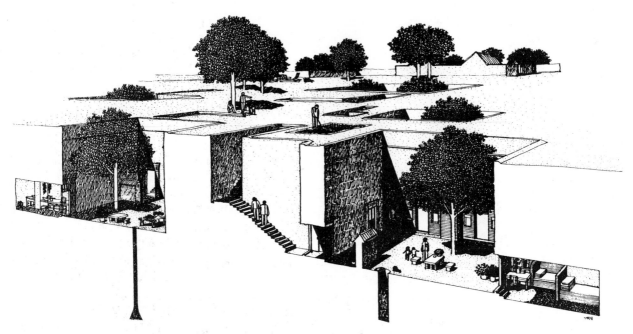

Figure 2.19. Perspective view of a sunken-courtyard *(aoting yaodong)* settlement in Henan province.

earth enclosing wall (Figure 2.23), just as is the case with the orthodox Beijing courtyard house. It contains not only a kitchen garden, a summer stove, and a flower garden but also a pigpen and a building for storage.

Each of the chambers, facing south and opening directly into the courtyard, has vertical sidewalls to a height of approximately 2 meters before arching. These arches are somewhat elliptical in shape; in other caves they may be semicircular, parabolic, flat, or even nearly pointed. Once completed, the walls are coated with a plaster of loess or loess and lime to slow the drying and flaking of the interior. The floor is earth which compacts readily to a bricklike texture. For most cave dwellings, a facade with a door, window, and upper vent is constructed of adobe bricks or tamped earth. This is usually accomplished before excavation begins (Figure 2.24). Sometimes a false arch is sculpted above the actual opening to sug-

gest greater height. A tile overhang may be added to the facade to reduce surface erosion and direct the flow of rain water away from the dwelling as seen in Plate 8.

In many areas of the mesa-like loessial plateau where cliffs are not available, peasants dig large rectangular pits often exceeding 100 square meters in size to form sunken courtyards *(aoting)* as shown in Figures 2.25 to 2.28. With sidewalls often exceeding 9 meters in depth, the sunken courtyard provides surfaces into which caves can be excavated. Very much like the common cliff dwellings discussed above, the resulting residential complex fronts on an open space and can accommodate a large extended family or even a hamlet of unrelated families. The courtyard serves as an important outdoor living space whenever the weather permits. Well-tended trees are grown in the courtyard, watered usually from a nearby well. Moreover, the courtyard is a secure

Figure 2.20. Exterior view of a *kaoshan yaodong* (cliffside cave dwelling) found northwest of Xian in Shaanxi province.

Figure 2.22. View of the kitchen and storage area of the dwelling shown in Figure 2.20.

Figure 2.21. Interior view of the vaulted-ceiling bedroom of the dwelling shown in Figure 2.20. A *kang* bed is located in front of the window.

Figure 2.23. Southeastern gate, surmounted with a roof of tile and wood, pierces the tamped earth wall which leads to the cliffside dwelling shown in Figure 2.20.

Figure 2.24. The arcuate facades of yet-to-be excavated cave dwellings are framed in wood and faced with brick. Lishi, Shanxi province.

"walled" compound in which to keep chickens, draft animals, and a pig. Since it is open to the sky, rain or snow as well as dirt drop directly into the courtyard. Sometimes a low parapet is placed along the top to retard rain from running over the edge.

In the typical *aoting,* some of the chambers are connected by doors as seen in Figure 2.26 and may even extend deeper than is the general rule with cliffside loessial dwellings. Shallow alcoves are common. Only one of the walls can face south and obtain direct sunlight and this exclusively during the summer months. In winter when the sun is low above the horizon, the depth of the courtyard effectively shades the whole space, a decided disadvantage. Generally no caves are dug on the southern rim of the sunken courtyard because it is always in shade even in summer.

Stairs, a ramp, or both are usually cut into the soil from this direction to provide access to the level land above, which is used for planting and for drying crops. In some areas, a village of caves may leave a landscape pocked with the deep indentations of courtyards.

There are positive features of subterranean dwellings, however. They use an abundantly available resource, the soil, and they provide at relatively low cost a dwelling that is warm in winter and cool in summer. The report of the 1982 Henan conference on loessial caves indicated that in winter when the outside temperature was 1 °C the temperature in cave dwellings reached 11.3 °C, almost 6 °C higher than in a common rural house. In summer, by contrast, with an outside temperature of 32 °C, the interior of the cave was only 21.4 °C while a shaded place in a surface

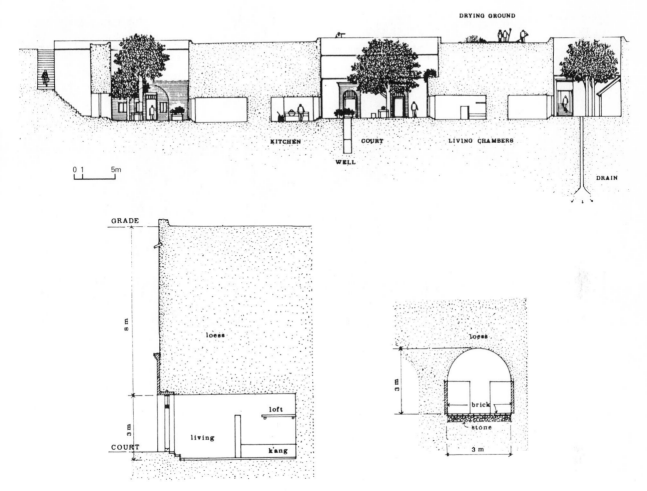

Figure 2.25. Scaled elevation views of an *aoting yaodong* complex in Henan province. Set approximately 11 meters beneath grade level, the courtyard and the 3-meter-high dwelling space have been carved from the loessial soil.

house was 29.6 °C (Zai 1984). In a region of continental climate with pronounced temperature extremes, this thermal performance is quite satisfactory. On the other hand, poor ventilation in the caves combined with the ambient temperature generally leads to quite high relative humidities in summer. The infrequent but powerful earthquakes that assault the region have sometimes devastated the loessial dwellings with great loss of life. The dwellings, however, can be rebuilt fairly

easily. Structural additions of brick or stone interior arches mitigate to a degree these dangers.

Recognizing positive and negative features of cave dwellings, some peasants in recent years as their resources permitted have built supplementary surface dwellings of adobe bricks or tamped earth near their caves. In these cases, the caves become the winter residence where with a stove and a *kang* bed a warm environment is assured. The surface dwelling provides an alternative

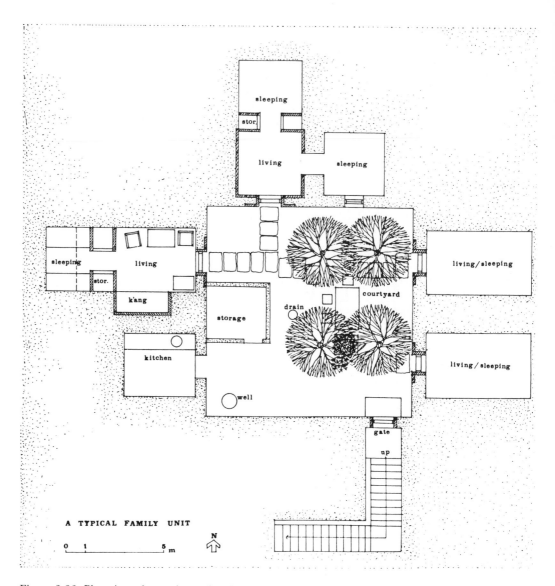

A TYPICAL FAMILY UNIT

0 1   5 m

N

Figure 2.26. Plan view of an *aoting yaodong* in Henan province shows living space dug into the north, east, and west sides of the courtyard. Entrance, as in surface houses, is from the south.

Figure 2.27. In appearance very much like cliffside caves, this sunken courtyard complex itself has been excavated to provide subterranean living space. Qianling, Shaanxi province.

sleeping and eating environment to use especially in summer where ventilation at the surface is more satisfactory. An aboveground dwelling in Shanxi province that is modeled after earth-sheltered housing is shown in Figure 2.29. An international conference on earth-sheltered housing was held in Beijing in fall 1985 as part of a search for ways to improve this significant housing resource.

SOUTHERN HOUSES

From the traditional perspective of north China, south China begins in the valley of the Changjiang (Yangzi River) and extends southward into the subtropical regions of the country. Covering more than half the area within the Great Wall, south China encompasses a variety of landscapes and climatic conditions that stretches across two of China's major river systems, the Changjiang and the Xijiang (West River). A moderate climate, including a long growing season and generally abundant rainfall, promotes the growth of diverse natural vegetation that is used in house construction. The fragmented topography of much of the south fostered the development of local traditions and nurtured local variations in many aspects of culture, including housing. This is as true in those areas along the southern border where Han Chinese intermingle with ethnic minority groups as it is where cultural differentiation is striking even among Han subgroups, as in Fujian and Guangdong provinces.

Migrating Chinese pioneers brought the basic rectangular northern housing layout to the south and adapted it to local conditions. A great deal of variation from area to area came about, reflecting not only differences in topography and economy but also the degree to which pioneers adopted local non-Chinese housing forms. Southern house builders in most areas had a broader range of building materials available to them than was the case in the north. Not only was timber more readily obtainable, but bamboo was so widely distributed and found in such variety that it became in many cases a substitute for wooden pillars. Where communities were defined by clan groupings, individual dwellings and ensembles of dwellings in villages developed patterns of crowded disorder

Figure 2.28. The four-faced courtyard provides common space for the household, including a small garden and space for washing and drying clothes. Qianling, Shaanxi province.

with shared walls joining the residences. Where terrain was especially uneven and canals plentiful, dwellings clung to the hillsides or reached over the water.

This section concentrates on rural dwellings in two areas of south China: those found in Fujian province along the southeast coast and those in the interior province of Sichuan. Other provinces within the region display local variations of patterns seen in these provinces such as the striking gables of dwellings in Jiangsu (Plate 7) and in Guangxi Zhuang Autonomous Region (Figure 2.30). Each of these areas has a long history of Chinese settlement.

The Dwellings of Fujian

Dwellings in Fujian tend to be larger and higher than common rural dwellings found in the north. This tendency is as true of basic rectangularly shaped houses of poorer peasants as it is of more substantial dwellings where the layout clearly is reminiscent of grander dwellings found in the cities of the north. Small-scale dwellings are usually rectangular and composed of three to five *jian* (bays) as in the north. Sometimes a second story is added, but more likely side buildings are attached if more space is required. Wherever resources permit, Fujian dwellings have been en-

Figure 2.29. A three-*jian* dwelling built after the fashion of cave dwellings. Lishi, Shanxi province.

Figure 2.30. Throughout southern China, roof lines and gable walls often present visually striking patterns. Rising above double sloped roofs in Guangxi Zhuang Autonomous Region are the "five peaks adoring heaven" gable style on the right and "cat crawling" gable style in the center. The common "firm mountain" style is on the left.

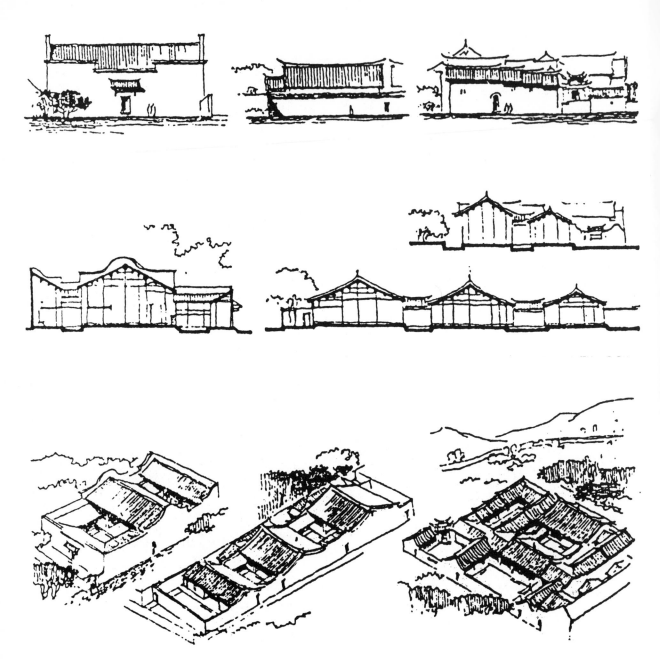

Figure 2.31. Three typical dwelling types found in Fujian province.

closed with walls. The need for protection arose out of building in remote mountainous areas where bandits were common. Walls have been retained as a principal element in the layout of rural dwelling even today even though the need is much less pronounced than in the past. As shown in Figure 2.31, the exterior appearance of dwellings of various sizes presents starkly whitewashed walls with only limited openings. While there might be multiple doors that could be bolted if needed, windows are entirely lacking in the outer walls.

Once inside the wall, however, the typical dwelling gives an open appearance, including a symmetrical layout and a defined axis, like that of the *siheyuan* or northern courtyard house found in cities such as Beijing. Interior space is composed of three parts: a courtyard (*tianjing* or "skywell"), a main hall *(tingtang),* and sleeping and cooking space. The courtyard, usually representing more than ten percent of the total area, is small in comparison with those in the north; serving principally to let in air for ventilation. Its size is typically restricted to limit direct sunlight from entering any of the rooms; this effect is enhanced with substantial roof overhangs (Figure 2.32). Complementary to the courtyard is the main hall, a building usually with a wide veranda connecting the courtyard to the hall through large doors and latticed windows. This veranda linking the courtyard and main hall provides intermediate space between the two, making possible the ventilation of the main hall even during heavy rain. It is possible to view both the inside and outside as joined since the activities in one typically flow into the other. Facing the door of the main hall is generally a long table for ceremonial purposes involving folk religion and respect for ancestors. Funerals and weddings take place in this combined interior and exterior space.

Figure 2.32. "Skywell" *(tianjing)* provides ventilation and light to the interior of a Fujian dwelling. Because of lengthy overhangs, the rays of the subtropical sun are prevented from entering the interior rooms.

Bedrooms, kitchens, and storage space in dwellings of this type are situated in rooms that parallel or run perpendicular to the *tingtang* or main hall. Figure 2.31 depicts posterior and lateral development from the basic core of the main hall. Following the principle of *qiantang houqin* (main room in front, bedrooms to the rear), most large peasant dwellings in northern and eastern Fujian have a structure built behind and parallel to the main hall for living purposes. This pattern is usually accompanied by side rooms (*pixie*) built along each of the walls that define the courtyard. It is not unusual for dwellings to grow laterally or horizontally to accommodate a large number of related persons. One rural dwelling in Xianyou *xian* in central Fujian began with a single building for one household and expanded to house one hundred individuals in ten related households (Huang 1982, 6). Peasants commonly declare that the house is an expression of family power, housing the *jiaqi* (family spirit) within its four walls. Folk beliefs limit the size of windows in the bedrooms of these residences to conserve the wealth of the household and to ensure that material possessions will not flow out from openings in the house (*cai buwailu*).

Wood framing is used in a majority of Fujian dwellings, often arranged in the interlocked *chuandou* structure discussed in the next chapter. For outer curtain walls, stone, brick, and tamped earth have been utilized extensively. In some areas along the coast, stone and brick are used in the same structure. Although the floor plan of a simple Fujian dwelling may not be strikingly dissimilar from one in north China, the use of a wood framing system results in stylistic elements that provide an elevation view more like that of a ceremonial building in the traditional style than an ordinary dwelling found in northern China. With a wood framing system and projecting eaves, pronounced curvature can be added to the pitched roof to serve the utilitarian function of carrying rainwater a great distance from the walls and foundation as well as furnishing the buoyant roof often seen as characteristic of Chinese architecture (Figure 2.33).

Figure 2.33. Large open-courtyard dwelling with extensions to the core building, including laterally placed side rooms to define the courtyard. The wooden framework permits curvature to the ridge line of the roof.

A variety of solutions are found in dwellings in Fujian and adjacent provinces to problems of ventilation and insulation from heat. These solutions include not only small courtyards, verandas, interior windows, and projecting eaves but also heat-radiating white walls, movable partitions to divide interior space, and in some cases double-layer tile roofs with an air space between (Lu 1978).

A uniquely distinctive dwelling type is found in the southwestern sections of Fujian and the adjoining northeastern parts of Guangdong province. Here walled multistoried villages of various sizes have been built by the Hakka, a Han Chi-

nese ethnic subgroup which migrated into the region from central China. Known for their clannishness and unwelcomed to the point of hostility by other Chinese settlers who preceded them, the Hakka often expropriated marginal land in the hilly areas of the interior. Drawing upon clan resources they built veritable multistoried forts of inexpensive tamped earth to house their communities. Layouts varied from square to rectangular to round shapes of different sizes (Figure 2.34). Those studied in greatest detail are located in the hilly areas of Yongding *xian* in Fujian (Liu Dunzhen 1957, 44–48, 121–126; Huang 1982 and 1984).

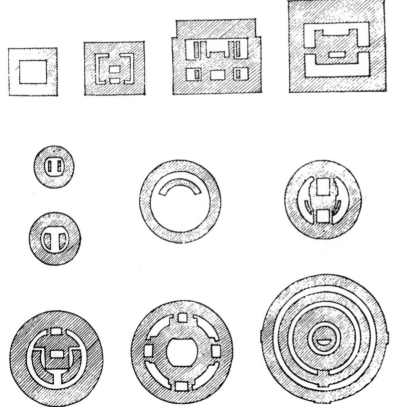

Figure 2.34. Basic rectangular and circular plans of Kejia (Hakka) multistoried dwellings with either three or four floors. Subsidiary buildings placed in the open courtyards may house cooking facilities, animal pens, or an ancestral hall.

Figure 2.35. Constructed of tamped earth nearly a meter thick, the walls of this four-story circular Kejia residential complex present a formidable appearance. Nanjing *xian,* Fujian province.

Figures 2.35 and 2.36 are exterior views of a medium-sized multistoried round joint dwelling found in Nanjing *xian* near the border with Guangdong province. Known colloquially as *tu lou* ("earthen building") or *yuan lou* ("round building"), such compounds typically are composed of a three or four-floor *chuandou* wood frame structure with load-bearing tamped earth or adobe walls that usually exceed a meter in thickness. The lower walls are windowless and pierced only by a single door. They encircle utilitarian rooms, including space for kitchens, livestock, and storage. In the circular plan, they open onto a courtyard containing a privy, adjacent pigsty, and chicken coop, as shown in Figure 2.37 of a larger *tulou* in adjacent Yongding *xian.* With the square plan, the same functions are carried out on the

lower level but in the center there is often a prominent courtyard and hall for guests and ceremonial activities. Stairways reach to the second floor, either windowless or with very small openings. This floor is used exclusively for the dry and secure storage of grain and other food stocks. The floors above are used for sleeping and usually have a number of small windows for ventilation and observation. Giving the appearance of a fortification, each complex indicates the ethnic isolation of the Hakka. The number of related households is suggested by the number of cooking areas (Huang 1984, 189–194).

The plan of a larger and more complex village compound is shown in Figure 2.38. Measuring some 52 meters in diameter, this circular walled village has four floors, the lower two of which

hall. In some compounds, as shown in Figure 2.39, the ancestral hall is placed in the center of the circle. As in the smaller dwellings discussed above, the remainder of the lower floors serve principally utilitarian needs with space for the reception of guests, kitchens, and an area to keep pigs and chickens. A separate and large latrine

Figure 2.36. A closeup view of the entrance of the Hakka dwelling shown in Figure 2.35, the battered walls and deep windows and door can be seen clearly.

have no windows. Set within the complex is a complementary two-storied building which has an open courtyard at its center. Both circular structures provide living space for an unidentified number of related individuals. Although circular, the building is laid out on an axis which passes through the southeastern door and across several courtyards before reaching the facing ancestral

Figure 2.37. Paved with stone, the interior courtyard opens the compound to the sky. At its center is space for the privy, pigsty, and chicken coop, as well as shade trees. Yongding *xian,* Fujian.

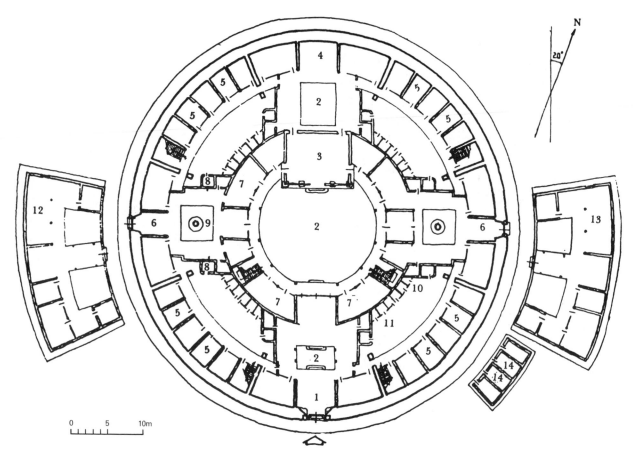

Figure 2.38. Kejia circular complex, Yongding *xian*, Fujian province. From the entrance (1), the axis passes through several courtyards (2) and a main hall (3) before reaching the ancestral hall (4). Extensive kitchens (5), side entrances (6), guest rooms (7), bathing facilities (8), a well (9), pigpens (10), and chicken coops (11) bring a degree of self-sufficiency to the complex. The large flanking outside buildings (12 and 13) contain equipment for milling rice. Nearby are the latrines (14).

building is placed outside the compound. The second floor of the outer ring is reserved for grain storage; the third and fourth floors are given over to bedrooms. The second floor of the inner ring is also used for sleeping. Access to all the upper-floor rooms is from balconies which ring the courtyard. Wells located within the walls provide a source of water. In addition to the substantial tamped earth walls which are mixed with lime for added strength, liberal amounts of timber and tile

are used in the construction of these Hakka dwellings.

Dwellings in Sichuan

With a population of more than 100 million spread densely across a rich subtropical basin and sparsely in surrounding mountains, Sichuan presents a cultural landscape of great variety. Rural houses reflect the long history of Chinese settlement and interaction with minority groups as well

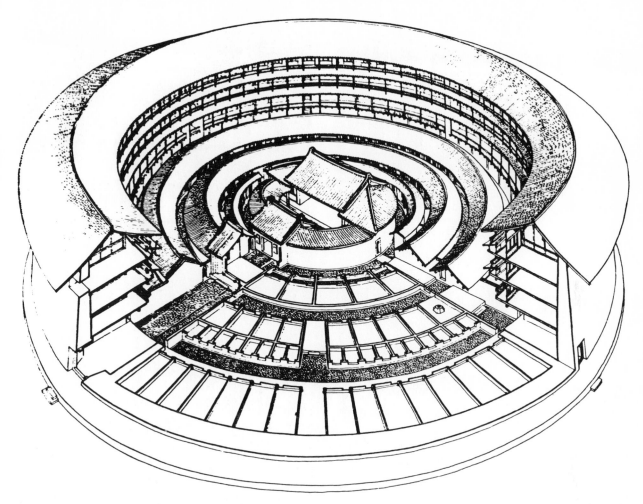

Figure 2.39. Perspective view of a large Kejia circular complex in Yongding *xian,* Fujian province. Similar to the one shown in Figure 2.36, this *tu lou* holds its ancestral hall in the center.

as the adaptation of local raw materials to ortho-dox northern housing patterns. No single general-ization can adequately address the variety of rural dwellings in this province that is nearly the size of Texas. This section therefore considers only a rep-resentative few of the common rural houses and their characteristics.

Large villages are not common in Sichuan; most of the rural population lives in isolated farm-

steads or in small hamlets. Farm dwellings are similar to those found in other subtropical areas of the country, such as those along the southeast coast, in their concern for adequate ventilation. Roofs of thick thatching or tile are necessary to shed the rainfall that generally exceeds 1,000 mil-limeters in most areas of the basin. Since bamboo and timber from the surrounding hill lands are abundant, frame structures are much more com-

Figure 2.40. Small rural house in the foothills of Emei mountain, western Sichuan province. With a substantial eaves overhang, the face of the dwelling is shaded during the summer.

Figure 2.41. L-shaped variant of basic Sichuan house, western Sichuan.

Figure 2.42. House in eastern Sichuan near Chongqing that is similar to the north China pattern.

mon than in north China. Walls of adobe, fired brick, and bamboo latticework as well as tamped earth are found. The building material depends largely on availability and the economic resources of the builder.

Whether a dwelling is a simple rectangle, L-shaped or U-shaped, or has an enclosed courtyard is related to peasant resources and need. In contrast with northern patterns, dwellings are not strictly sited facing south but rather are built in accordance with local topographic and microclimatic conditions. Figure 2.40 portrays a house in the foothills of Emei mountain near Chengdu. Essentially similar in layout to the three-bay dwelling on the north China plain, this basic rectangle differs, however, in the substantial overhang which shades the facade of the house. Further, unlike the north China house which invites sunlight into the interior with large windows in front, this dwelling has smaller windows which are further shaded by tobacco hanging on the eaves. Small raised windows on the far side facilitate cross ventilation. The privy is located off to the side as are a lean-to storage shed, a pigsty, and chicken coop. No wall or fence divides the house from the abutting fields which come almost to the front door. Figure 2.41 shows a variant of this house with an L-shaped extension to provide added sleeping space for a married son. It too sits within the fields and is defined in the landscape by a thicket of bamboo which provides shade and a windbreak.

In some cases, as shown in Figure 2.42, dwellings duplicate houses on the north China plain and do not recognize the humid and hot conditions of Sichuan. This figure depicts a small cluster of adobe and tamped earth houses on the outskirts of Chongqing in eastern Sichuan. Neither a prominent overhang nor a plastered wall protects the earthen walls from downpours. The tile roofs are a qualitative improvement over readily available thatch, but there is a curious lack of side or rear windows for cross ventilation. The absence of these windows might be seen as an asset in the north, but in Sichuan it represents a shortcoming in terms of comfort.

SUMMARY

Sharing a common building tradition that finds its fullest expression in palaces and temples, common rural houses mirror as well local environmental and social conditions. The sensitivity of Han peasants to diverse natural environments in a nation of 9,560,900 square kilometers has led to a variety of dwelling forms that help to differentiate a cultural mosaic that includes significant non-Han elements as well. Acknowledged building forms have been adapted to meet the specific requirements of site, available materials, and family circumstances.

Found in compact villages and hamlets or free-standing in dispersed settlements, rural houses usually take a rectangular form emphasizing the horizontal dimension even when multistoried. In front elevation, the preference is for symmetry; an apparent imbalance often reveals a dwelling in the process of growth. There is an additive quality to peasant houses, guided by notions of hierarchy and precedence, that gives spatial definition to the human relationships which it contains and expresses. The utilization of interior space is only broadly differentiated with multiple uses of each room. Vernacular Chinese architecture in its variant forms represents a composite idiom that goes beyond mere shelter to express shared values within the folk culture.

CHAPTER *3*

Construction of the Rural Chinese House

TRADITIONAL houses in China have been less designed than merely built. Rural dwellings largely have been constructed with the accumulated experience of peasants themselves and supplemented when necessary by the work of local craftsmen. Guiding principles derived from inherited ways did govern form and structure, as it did in monumental architecture, but usually there was much more flexibility in adapting these axioms to local housing needs than was the case with religious and ceremonial buildings. This chapter examines the structural components of the Chinese rural house, emphasizing materials and means of construction.

FOUNDATIONS

Chinese dwellings universally lack basements and, except for certain regional housing types identified with ethnic minorities, the contemporary Chinese house is rarely elevated on a platform in the manner of Japanese and Southeast Asian houses. Instead, the Chinese dwelling generally sits squarely on compacted earth at grade level or slightly elevated. Since only the poorest

houses are built without a foundation, the soil of the base and walls both absorb and hold moisture.

Tamped podiums or foundations (*jichu*) were first utilized during the Shang dynasty (roughly 1600–1100 B.C.) in order to reduce dampness and provide a firm base for the heavy structures to be placed upon them. Coupled with pipes and troughs, the pounded earth podium has been widespread in dwellings of all types and gives evidence of concern for a dry and secure base. Such sensitivity to the warmth of the earth and the need to control its moisture content no doubt was appropriate in neolithic and subsequent settlements on the north China plain and in many areas later occupied by Chinese peasants. Yet Chinese migrants carried with them this predilection for construction directly on the ground even in areas where its appropriateness was questionable—not only in areas of southern China but throughout peninsular Southeast Asia where raised dwellings on piles reduced humidity by ventilation from beneath. Sometimes the walls are set upon a base of cut stone or fired brick placed on the tamped earth foundation, especially in wet areas, as is shown in the raised stone base of a new dwelling in Guangxi Zhuang Autonomous Region (Figure 3.1). The stone or brick can be extended beyond the walls to mitigate the flow of water from the roof.

THE STRUCTURAL FRAMEWORK

In enclosing and spanning space, Chinese builders confronted universal problems: "In the same way that the house responds to the physical stresses of climate—heat, cold, humidity, radiation, and light—it must respond structurally to the mechanical stresses—gravity, wind, rain, and snow" (Rapoport 1969, 104). The builder's response to these problems is to a large degree governed by available materials and the inherited tradition that derives from experience.

At the most basic level, the structural framework of a Chinese dwelling depends on whether the walls are load-bearing *(chengzhong)* or not. Both conditions are more common in Chinese construction than is generally acknowledged in studies of Chinese architecture. In detailing the structure of Chinese buildings, including residences, primacy is usually given to the presence of a wooden framework supporting the roof. In such

Figure 3.1. For a raised foundation in some humid areas, a stone base elevates the brick dwelling above the low ground level. Earth is compacted within to serve as the floor. Near Guilin, Guangxi Zhuang Autonomous Region.

cases, the walls are mere curtains and bear no load, much as in contemporary skyscraper construction. That these wooden frameworks are a significant characteristic of traditional Chinese architecture is not disputed. Indeed, the architectural uniqueness of Chinese palaces, temples, and large residences derives essentially from the wooden skeletons which brought them to life. Still, most rural buildings in the countryside have not met such developed standards, depending instead on load-bearing walls to support the roof and, in some cases, even upper stories.

Load-Bearing Walls

Load-bearing walls are found not only in buildings made of tamped earth but in those of adobe and kiln brick as well. *Hangtu,* the tamped earth method of construction, has been used for raising the walls of houses and those surrounding compounds throughout Chinese history, as shown in Figure 3.2. A method arising out of an economy of scarcity, as well as the ubiquity of suitable soils, the building of tamped earth walls has been practiced throughout the country (Shan 1981). The method is used widely even today in the People's Republic of China.

Known in French as *pise de terre,* the *hangtu* technique involves piling freshly dug earth into a battered caisson consisting of a pair of tapering V-shaped supports reaching perhaps 4 meters in height that are framed on their long sides by movable wooden timbers or slats (Figures 3.3 and 3.4). In order to increase its bearing strength, the earth is then pounded with rammers until it is sufficiently firm to support the ramming of another layer above it. The timber frame is raised, leveled, and clamped into place and the process repeated until the wall reaches the desired height. Once the frame is removed, the wall is left with a corrugated surface which can be smoothed if desired. If the soil does not bind itself sufficiently, locally suitable materials such as oils and straw

Figure 3.2. Traditional drawing of the method of raising a wall using the tamped earth *(hangtu)* technique of construction.

Figure 3.3. Utilizing a traditional sloping frame and rammers, workers raise a wall of tamped earth in the loessial highlands of south central Shaanxi.

A pictorial and detailed description of variant *hangtu* methods of wall construction in wetter areas of eastern China, differing somewhat from the description presented here, is offered by Rudolf P. Hommel in *China at Work* (1937, 286–296).

Load-bearing walls of adobe or kiln-dried brick are found throughout China (Figures 3.7 and 3.8). While adobe bricks have been the materials used generally by poorer peasants, fired bricks always have been preferred by those who could

Figure 3.4. Reaching almost 3 meters in height, the battered wall is left with a corrugated appearance.

may be added to ensure adequate compaction. To reduce the transmission of moisture from the ground to the walls, a base of stones or rubble may be laid first as shown in Figure 3.5. Stone is sometimes placed at intervals within the wall for the same purpose (Figure 3.6). Where the roof is to join the walls, a row of tiles similarly can be set to minimize the rotting of roof timbers.

The process is vividly described in the *Shijing* (Book of Songs), since the second century B.C. known as one of the Five Classics:

> Dead straight was the plumb line,
> The planks were lashed to hold the earth;
> . . . .
> They tilted in the earth with a rattling,
> They pounded it with a dull thud,
> They beat the walls with a loud clang,
> They pared and chiselled them with a
>   faint *p'ing, p'ing;*
> The hundred cubits all rose.
>
> [Waley 1937, 248–249]

Figure 3.5. Stone laid at the base of a tamped earth wall to retard the movement of moisture from the earth; near Kunming, Yunnan province.

Figure 3.7. Adobe bricks form the load-bearing walls of this large dwelling in Guangxi Zhuang Autonomous Region. An improved burnt-tile roof has been added.

Figure 3.6. In addition to a stone base, the walls of this dwelling near Hangzhou, Zhejiang province, have layers of broken rock placed at intervals in the walls in order to reduce the transmission of moisture.

Figure 3.8. Built essentially as a duplicate in style and size of the adobe dwelling in Figure 3.7, this adjacent house is of fired brick.

afford them. As resources permitted, sometimes an adobe wall would be replaced brick by brick with improved fired bricks. Together with tamped earth walls, adobe bricks constituted nearly fifty percent of all farm buildings in China in the early

1930s, most of these in the north (Buck 1937, 443). The extensive use of adobe bricks traditionally was necessitated because of the need to conserve the available fuel for cooking and heating rather than firing bricks. Using the accessible earth around them, peasants at very low cost could easily build a house. When poorly formed, however, earthen walls could "melt down overnight" from the pounding of a heavy downpour or from flooding, according to observations in Sichuan province (Spencer 1947, 261). Generally it was less the loss of the dwelling which brought suffering to the peasants than the ruin of stored grain and seed. Under extreme conditions of famine, the peasant might be compelled to destroy even more of the house to obtain the wooden rafters which could be sold to procure food.

The methods of brick manufacture have local variants that nonetheless follow common traditional practices as shown in Figure 3.9 from the seventeenth century technological manual *Tiangong kaiwu* ("The creations of nature and man"). In the semiarid loessial areas of western Shanxi, near Lishi, brick making is a wholly manual activity not unlike that shown in the Ming manual. Figure 3.10 shows the compaction by hand of the siltlike soil, dug from walls of earth using a mattock, into double nonreleasable molds. After trimming with a bow-shaped wire cutter, the individual adobe bricks are left to cure in the April sun (Figures 3.11 and 3.12). Digging in the autumn near Lanzhou, Gansu province, in similar loessial soil which has been moistened by summer rains, peasants are able to utilize rammers similar to those employed in the construction of *hangtu* walls in an effort to increase compaction (Figure 3.13 and Plate 11). In this way it is possible to draw on marginal soils found along roads and railways, transforming the earth into hardened bricks which can be carried easily to building sites. Utilizing fine clay soils transported by wind as well as water, variants of these practices are in use throughout the country. In northwest China, coal dust and peat are mixed with local soil to produce a black brick (Figure 3.14). It has

been suggested that the practice increases the moisture resistance of such bricks, allowing them to be used as a kind of vapor barrier for floors and foundation stones (Jin 1982, 51).

In areas of irrigated rice fields, bricks may be cut directly from the field itself. Because of siltation of paddy fields over time, proper water depth

Figure 3.9. As depicted in the seventeenth-century manual *Tiangong kaiwu*, bricks are fashioned in wooden frames from readily available soil. A wire bow is used to cut off the surplus soil before the bricks are left to dry.

Figure 3.10. Dug from the hills of Lishi, western Shanxi, loessial soil is pounded by hand into a nonreleasable mold to make two bricks.

Figure 3.12. The pair of uniform adobe bricks are dumped from the mold to dry in the sun.

Figure 3.11. Utilizing a wire bow to cut the excess soil smooth, the brickmaker uses a method similar to that shown in the *Tiangong kaiwu* diagram.

is maintained by lowering the floor of the field about once every ten years. Carried out usually during the fall, the newly harvested field is plowed and then harrowed. The fields are then either flooded from canals or allowed to become puddled after a heavy rain. Once evaporation has reduced the moisture content of the soil to the consistency of putty, brick-size sections of soil with a thickness of approximately 15 centimeters are cut from the floor of the field using a spade. The process is shown in Figures 3.15, 3.16, and Plate 12. Here, near Guilin in southern China, the cut portions of the paddy floor are carried to a wooden frame where they are pounded with the feet to a common shape and left to air dry. Later stacked and left to cure on a bed of straw for several weeks in

Figure 3.13. Using hand rammers to compress the soil in releasable molds, adobe bricks are formed and pounded from local loessial soil to the west of Lanzhou, Gansu province.

the autumn sun, the bricks can then be used for house building. Unlike the heat of summer which would dry the bricks too quickly, thus forming cracks, the less intense sun of autumn assures a more satisfactory building material.

It has been the practice in north China to leave the pounded earth or adobe walls bare, presenting a soft brown tone that links the earth and the buildings above. Elsewhere in the country, a mixture of mud and straw and perhaps lime is sometimes added as a finish to reduce rainwash. In southern China, this plaster is often whitewashed

to reflect the sun and function as a thermal regulator. Owing to the weight of the upper wall and the roof, few windows or doors are normally placed in load-bearing adobe or tamped earth buildings. Windows and door, moreover, are usually placed only in the front wall which, in many parts of central and southern China, may be constructed of wood to allow for larger windows.

Although brick making has a history of at least two millennia in China, only about twenty percent of dwellings surveyed in the early 1930s had walls of fired brick. Fired brick construction was

Figure 3.14. These thin bricks are made of coal dust and mud. They are used as a kind of vapor barrier for floors and foundation stones in Xinjiang Uygur Autonomous Region.

more common in areas of prosperity, especially in southern China, and more than twice as likely to be found where the farmstead was a large one rather than small (Buck 1937, 443). Today brick kilns *(zhuanyao)* of various sizes are seen throughout the countryside and are used in the local production of fired bricks. For the most part, the mud used in the making of such bricks is taken from the banks of rivers, canals, or even from irrigated fields where the water has sorted the soil by size and texture. It is kneaded, moistened with water, and molded in a wooden frame (Figures 3.17 and 3.18). Releasable and nonreleasable brick molds are used to give shape to the viscous soil. Whatever clay protrudes above the mold is sliced off with a cutting bow, formed by a wire

Figure 3.15. To remove accumulated siltation, soil is dug from the floor of a paddy field softened with water. Working from two directions, the peasants use a flat shovel to move the earth to the portable shaping frame. Guangxi Zhuang Autonomous Region.

Figure 3.16. The moist soil is placed into a shaping frame and pressed into place by the worker's foot. The bamboo handles are used to raise the mold and reposition it.

Figure 3.17. Bricks which are to be fired are prepared more carefully than are adobe bricks to insure compaction and even drying. A releasable mold is used by this brickmaker. Guangxi Zhuang Autonomous Region.

Figure 3.18. A wire cutting bow is used to trim the brick to size. Each brick is set on its own pallet for moving.

held taut by a pliant branch. Individually formed bricks are then piled on edge, covered with straw to keep off the sun, and left to dry for about a week before firing (Figure 3.19). Unlike adobe bricks, those prepared in this fashion can be made year round since they will be fired.

In preparation for firing, brick-lined kilns are dug into the earth and faced with rough stone before being filled from an opening in the top with layers of sun-dried bricks, fuel, and rough stone to hold the heat (Figure 3.20). Once filled, the roof of the kiln is plastered over; only a draft hole is left to regulate the fire beneath. Using coal,

Figure 3.19. Bricks are carefully stacked and let to air dry for a week before being fired.

comprehensive treatment of brick bonds and plaster can be found in Hommel (1937, 278–293).

Stone generally has not been used as a building material in China to a degree that matches its availability. Stone dwellings, such as those shown in Figures 3.22, and 3.23, are found usually in mountainous areas where the soil itself is quite thin or along the southeast coast in Fujian (Yu 1985, 6; Lee 1978). In other remote areas where

Figure 3.20. Dug into the earth, this brick kiln reaches 3 meters above ground level. The bricks to be fired are placed in the kiln from the top which is then plastered over. The firing hole in the center of the figure is linked to a draft hole on the other side to control the heat. Near Guilin, Guangxi Zhuang Autonomous Region.

grain stalks, or boughs of available trees, the fire is maintained for approximately twenty-four hours. Subsequently, the kiln is sealed and allowed to cool over a period of up to a week. The hot bricks may be doused with water to cool them, producing a gray brick preferred in some areas. The color of the brick generally reflects the soil from which it is made. A variety of bonding patterns and mortar, composed of lime and sand, are utilized throughout China. Figure 3.21 shows an adobe brick wall with a common bond and plaster composition. Often only used in foundation walls that need to withstand the onrush of water, this bond is composed of a course of stretchers followed by a course of headers which are stood on edge. The stretchers break joints with one another to increase the strength of the wall. Other common box bond patterns are shown in Figure 2.10, 3.7, and 3.8. The plaster is a mixture of mud, lime, and vegetable fiber, spread on in layers. A

Figure 3.21. Mud, lime, and vegetable fiber plaster is used on this exterior wall. The brick bond is especially rigid, one in which a course of stretchers is topped by a course of headers stood on edge; the courses of stretchers break joints with one another. Found here in the semiarid area of Shaanxi province, the bond is utilized extensively throughout the country.

large trees are easily available, roughly hewn logs are stacked much in the fashion of simple log houses in America (Liang 1980, 243). The isolated well-watered areas of the southwest, especially Yunnan, as well as in Xinjiang in the northwest are locales where log houses are still being built (Figure 3.24).

Nonload-Bearing Walls

Viewed from the perspective of their basic components, nonload-bearing wall structures in China

are not strikingly different from standard post-and-lintel systems used in the west. Both utilize vertical pillars or posts upon which horizontal members (beams, girders, or lintels) are placed. The horizontally placed members collect the weight of the roof and floors placed upon them and transfer the forces to the vertical elements which carry them to the ground. Where loads are supported in such a fashion, the walls become nonload-bearing curtains or screens, serving to enclose rather than support.

Wood framework construction *(mugoujia jiegou)* is often viewed as an axiomatic element in the Chinese architectural tradition and is used in monumental buildings of various sizes, as shown in Figure 3.25, as well as in residences. When such structural systems are examined it is seen that the truly unique components are those which are placed above the pillars *(zhu);* it is these elements which give definition to the roof rather than the vertical supports themselves. Accordingly, the variants of these structural systems are

Figure 3.22. Stone, plastered with a mud and lime mixture, is used to build dwelling walls in an area lacking wood and good soil in northern Shanxi province.

Figure 3.23. Near Qijiashan, Jiangsu province in central China, some dwellings are made of cut stone.

Figure 3.24. In some areas of northwest and southwest China where forests are extensive, the logs are stacked and a mud plaster applied to form simple log houses. Usually built by ethnic minorities, they are sometimes constructed by Han Chinese as well. Northern slopes of Tianshan, Xinjiang Uygur Autonomous Region.

Figure 3.25. Orthodox column-and-beam construction is shown in this newly raised building in Xuanwumen Park in Beijing.

not examined here but will be considered later in the discussion of roofs.

Nonload-bearing walls, used with wood framework construction, may be of tamped earth, adobe, fired brick, bamboo, wattle and daub, or other locally available material such as stone (Figure 3.26). Curtains of tamped earth, adobe, or fired brick are arranged between the vertical supports of the structure, allowing relative freedom in the placement of windows and doors. Wall materials of vegetative origin, such as bamboo, kaoliang, or cornstalks, traditionally have been most common in central, southeastern, and southwestern China (Figure 3.27). Where bamboo is used for walling, it typically is split and interlaced at a 90-degree angle. Mud or mud-and-lime plaster can be spread on either or both sides to make the wall tight to air and moisture. Dwellings of this type seen in Sichuan or Jiangxi have been described as reminiscent of vernacular dwellings in England and Germany (Spencer 1947, 262). Sometimes a reed or finely split bamboo matting replaces latticed bamboo walls. Buck's survey of fifty years ago showed such walls as most common in southwestern China where they were found in sixty-two percent of the buildings. Elsewhere in the south, according to Buck, woven walls competed with adobe and tamped earth according to local conditions as the most common walling. Although sawn timber has never been widely used to form walls in humble Chinese dwellings, in the larger residences of the wealthy much of the facade might be of sawn wood.

In simple dwellings, the pillars which form the vertical elements of the rising superstructure are not firmly anchored to the tamped earth foundation but rest upon roughly hewn stone pedestals (*zhuchu* or *zhuzuo*). More substantial residences may have pedestals of carved stone in a variety of forms, including octagonal shapes representing the *bagua* or Eight Trigrams. Stone pedestals protect the wooden pillars from dampness and the encroachment of termites.

The beams, pillars, and stone pedestals, all set upon a compacted foundation, permit a resonance to the structure. Especially appropriate in areas of earthquakes, amid "the falling heavens and cracking earth," this arrangement enables horizontal movements to be countered by a flexible structure. Furthermore, because the pillars are not anchored to the ground they are able to move with the tremors rather than against them. Although the walls themselves might fall, the integrity of the wood framework would most likely be maintained. The framework represented the most difficult component to replace; the intervening walls could be reconstructed fairly easily from local earth.

Figure 3.26. The wood frame of this dwelling supports the roof directly. A 1.5 meter stone wall serves as a high foundation wall for the plastered woven bamboo curtain wall which rises above it. Shangtianzhu, near Hangzhou, Zhejiang province.

Figure 3.27. Walls of vegetative origin have been woven to cover this small dwelling in Hubei province.

Figure 3.28. New flat-roofed dwelling near Zhaoxian, Hebei province. Except for the doors and windows, no wood was used in the construction.

ROOF STRUCTURES, PROFILES, AND COMPOSITION

The roof *(wuding)* of a Chinese building may range from a purely functional covering to one exemplifying a powerful elegance. This section reviews Chinese roofing systems starting with the simplest and progressing to the more complex types.

Structural Support of the Roof

Where the walls are load-bearing as in much of the poorer *hangtu* or adobe dwellings and some fired brick structures, the roof profile may be flat, have a single slope, or a double slope (Figures 3.28 and 3.29). The horizontal timbers, called purlins, are set directly upon the gable walls to form a simple structure termed *yingshanjialin*

Figure 3.29. The wooden purlins and rafters will be set directly on the brick walls of this single-slope-roofed dwelling near Datong, northern Shanxi.

("firm mountain gable wall with purlin framework"). Where the wall is of adobe or tamped earth composition, a layer of tile or stone fragments is usually placed between the earthen wall and the timbers to reduce rotting, but it serves no structural function.

To supplement the support of the walls where a broad space is spanned, wooden or brick columns that do not reach above the height of the walls may be placed in the interior of a dwelling. Found especially in Xizang (Tibet) and Xinjiang among non-Han ethnic minorities, the resulting framing system is one in which purlins are laid along the tops of the walls and the interior columns, supporting directly closely spaced rafters (Figure 3.30). This type is called the *miliang pingding* or purlins and rafters flat-roofed framing system. A flat-roofed dwelling that is appropriate in areas of limited rainfall results, which is nonetheless easily deformed by the weight of the roof and the decomposition of the wooden members as seen in the deteriorating structure in Figure 3.31.

Where logs are stacked to form walls and directly support the load of the roof, a *jinggan* or "well frame" is formed. Found in the more remote upland areas in southwestern and northwestern China, this frontier type dwelling has been used by Han as well as ethnic minority builders. The simple log cabin located in the northern slopes of the Tianshan in northern Xinjiang shown in Figure 3.24 was of this type. Comprising only a small single room, each of the interlocked log walls rose to a common height before a stack of logs of decreasing length was added to define the double sloping roof. More complex log dwellings, sometimes with two storys and multiple rooms that express features that are distinctly Chinese, have been documented in the mountainous areas of Yunnan province in southwestern China (Figure 3.32).

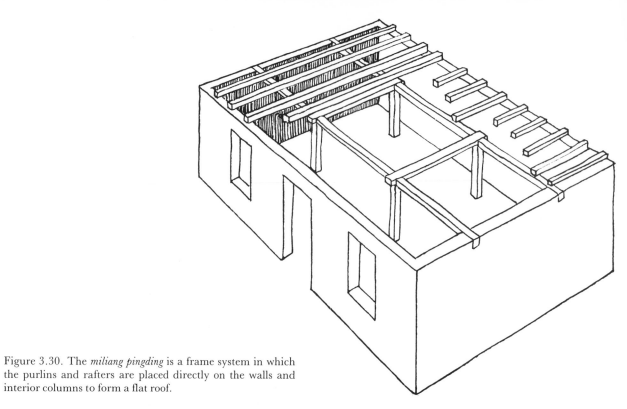

Figure 3.30. The *miliang pingding* is a frame system in which the purlins and rafters are placed directly on the walls and interior columns to form a flat roof.

Figure 3.31. If the supporting columns are not spaced closely enough together, the heavy roof of a *miliang pingding* structure may sag. Tulufan, Xinjiang Uygur Autonomous Region.

Figure 3.32. *Jinggan* or "well frame" log houses are found in the upland areas of northwest and southwest China. Especially in Yunnan province, this type often exhibits distinctly Chinese roof lines.

It is the additive features placed above the the vertical pillars and horizontal beams of wood framing systems which signal the unique and original contribution of the Chinese architectural tradition and define the characteristic Chinese roof. Based principally upon the means by which the various rising elements are interlocked, two distinct framing systems can be identified: *tailiang* (also called *liangzhu*), or pillars and beams and *chuandou,* or pillars and transverse tie beams. The repertoire of elements utilizing these framing systems in fashioning the roof structures of temples, palaces, and other types of monumental architecture is well described (Steinhardt 1984a and 1984b; Glahn 1981; Liang 1984, 11–12).

Wood framework systems for rural dwellings include elementary pillar-and-post construction as well as more elaborate techniques which mimic and rival those of temples and palaces. In no other feature of Chinese housing is the prosperity of the owner so clearly expressed. Figure 3.33 depicts a traditional small dwelling on the north China plain with earthen walls and, like the dwelling shown in Figure 2.8, a very limited amount of timber. The section view indicates corner posts only on the facade of the building; these posts support beams which rise at a modest slope to seats on the back wall. The beams support five purlins (*lin, linzi* or *hengtiao*) upon which are placed rafters (*chuanzi*) and the roof covering. Except for the south-facing facade, which includes a door and whose upper half is composed of wood, the walls are unbroken as protection against the prevailing northerly winds.

A similar pillar-and-post frame found in the area of Zhengzhou, Henan province, permits a

Figure 3.33. Shed-type roof supported in the front by posts and in the back by the wall. This dwelling is located in the southern suburbs of Beijing.

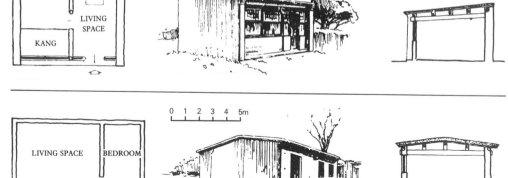

Figure 3.34. A modest *liangzhu* (pillar and post) dwelling with a layered composition double-sloped roof, Zhengzhou, Henan province.

double-sloping saddle profile to the roof (Figure 3.34). Short posts (*guazhu*) lift the purlins and define the peaked slope of the roof. Otherwise the dwelling is as modest as the one just described. Both of these structures economize on the use of timber and are common in areas of limited woodland where wood is expensive. Similar roofs found in north and central China include those where the front or rear is raised slightly with a longer shedlike slope completing the roof. In some areas of the northeast a rounded roof profile is made possible by using the same elemental pillar-and-beam system with short posts set upon the beam to give the roof shape (see Figure 2.11).

The roof profile of the *tailiang* system appears similar to that resulting from the truss systems used to define western roofs. Unlike the truss, however, which is based upon triangularly positioned segments, the cross section of the developed *tailiang* system is a composition of beams of progressively shorter lengths placed one above the other to define the slope of the roof, as can be seen in the profile of a farmhouse being dismantled near Beijing (Figure 3.35). Characteristic of *taili-*

Figure 3.35. Beams and queen posts support this roof on a rural dwelling being dismantled in the northern suburbs of Beijing.

ang construction is the use of only a small number of pillars, often only corner posts to carry the weight of the beams, upon which the purlins, then the rafters, and finally the roofing material rest. The spanning beams collect the forces from the roof structure and transfer them to the vertical pillars.

Unlike the rigid triangulated truss system which provides a V-shaped roof profile, the *tailiang* framing system and that of the *chuandou,* to be discussed next, give greater design possibilities to the roofline (Figure 3.36). By altering the placement of struts and purlins atop the beams, even pronounced curvature can be introduced into the roof profile. The straighter and less graceful roofline traditionally has been found on more humble dwellings while as a signature of status a freer design was used on residences of those with more means. Figure 3.37 presents a modest *tailiang* structure with two sets of beams, four purlins, and a ridgepole supporting a typical roof.

The *chuandou* framing system differs from the *tailiang* system in three important ways: The roof purlins which support the rafters and roof itself rest directly on the pillars rather than on beams or struts; the number of pillars is greater; and *chuan-fang,* horizontal tie-beam members, are mortised directly into or tenoned through the columns to form an interlocked matrix. In this framing system, the weight of the roof is carried from the purlins directly to each pillar and then to the ground. The great number of pillars is necessitated by the fact that individually each pillar is weakened by the grooves or slots which are mortised to hold the horizontal tie beams. This weakening leads obviously to the increase in the number of pillars and decrease in their spacing in comparison with the *tailiang* system in which none of the pillars is made less stable by cutting. By multiplying the vertical and horizontal members, the timber used then may be of smaller diameter and therefore less expensive than that necessary for a *tailiang* frame.

Well developed by the Han period, the *chuandou* system is still widely used today, especially in

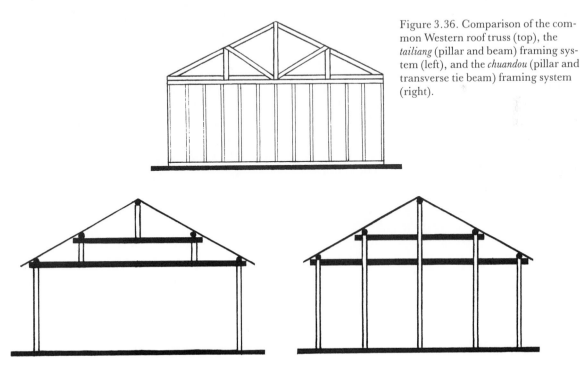

Figure 3.36. Comparison of the common Western roof truss (top), the *tailiang* (pillar and beam) framing system (left), and the *chuandou* (pillar and transverse tie beam) framing system (right).

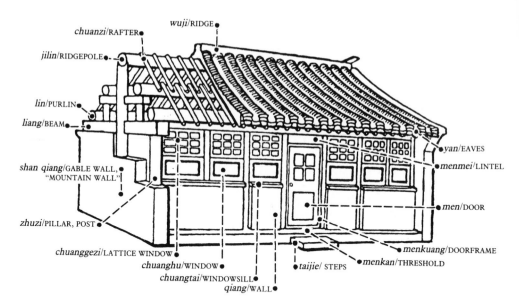

wuji/RIDGE
chuanzi/RAFTER
jilin/RIDGEPOLE
lin/PURLIN
liang/BEAM
yan/EAVES
menmei/LINTEL
shan qiang/GABLE WALL, "MOUNTAIN WALL"
men/DOOR
zhuzi/PILLAR, POST
menkuang/DOORFRAME
chuanggezi/LATTICE WINDOW
menkan/THRESHOLD
chuanghu/WINDOW
taijie/STEPS
chuangtai/WINDOWSILL
qiang/WALL

Figure 3.37. A simple *tailiang* framing system and the basic components of a Chinese dwelling.

southern China, as shown in Figure 3.38 and Plate 13. In this house, the frame includes five pillars running from the ground and notched at the top to hold the purlins. An unusual arrangement is that of the two supplementary short pillars flanking the central pillar. The horizontal *chuanfang* are shown mortised into the pillars, at once stabilizing and weakening them. Intersecting wooden tie rods and upper loft supports are also tied into the pillars by mortise and tenon. A broad overhang is indicated by the thrust of the forward *chuanfang*. In some cases, the *chuandou* framework is used on the gable ends but is supplemented by *tailiang* frames in the interior of larger dwellings (Liu Dunzhen 1980, 6). It also may be used in conjunction with load-bearing walls, as shown in Figure 3.39, of a brick dwelling in Guangxi Zhuang Autonomous Region. Here, the *chuandou* structure serves as support for the purlins because of the width of interior space. The placement of the wooden frame divides the space into *jian*.

Both the *tailiang* and *chuandou* framing systems

permit a high degree of flexibility and freedom of design—essential for peasant dwellings that normally undergo alteration and expansion as fortune allows. Equidistant spacing and equal height of pairs of pillars simplify and standardize the building process, making possible a surprising degree of modularization and even prefabrication. Depth, length, and height of a dwelling are determined according to local practices and can be altered to reflect changing circumstances. Depth is regulated by the number and spacing of roof purlins. In *tailiang* structures, seen in the progression of Figure 3.40, the number of purlins, which fixes the depth, varies from three to nine even with as few as two pillars. With *chuandou* frames, the number of pillars would increase to match the number of purlins. The length of a dwelling depends on the number of transverse frame supports; its height is governed by the length of the pillars and placement of floor joists.

Each front-to-back frame, whether *tailiang* or *chuandou*, encloses areal units known as *jian* or bays that are individually defined by adjacent pil-

depth is made possible by increasing the number of purlins. With purlins spaced 1 to 1½ meters apart, the depth sometimes exceeds 10 meters, allowing the interior space to be divided into front and back rooms.

The adaptability of these framing systems is evident also in the building of taller dwellings in central and southern China. Throughout these regions, rooms often exceed 4 meters in height. At once improving ventilation, increased height also makes possible the construction of lofts (gelou) for secure and dry storage as well as for sleeping. Such ancillary lofts are set upon joists which have been notched into the chuandou frame. Similarly, a second story can be added in areas of limited

Figure 3.38. The *chuandou* framing system as seen in new house construction at the foot of Emei mountain, western Sichuan.

lars. Earlier mention was made of a three-*jian* dwelling in north China which was constructed using four front-to-back wooden frames that divided the space into three *jian*, each 3 to 4 meters wide. In north China, the depth is normally shallow to permit the low winter sun to penetrate the room. The depth rarely exceeds 5 meters; normally there are only two pairs of corner pillars and three purlins. If the roof is inordinately heavy, a supplementary pair of purlins might be raised above the beam on short posts. Rural houses in southern China normally recede to greater depth, usually exceeding 5 meters. The

Figure 3.39. A load-bearing brick wall supports the roof purlins on both ends of this house. In the interior, a *chuandou* wood frame is placed between the gable walls. Guilin, Guangxi Zhuang Autonomous Region. This is a rear view of the dwelling presenting a simple and less carefully laid brick pattern to the wall than is the case with the front and side walls.

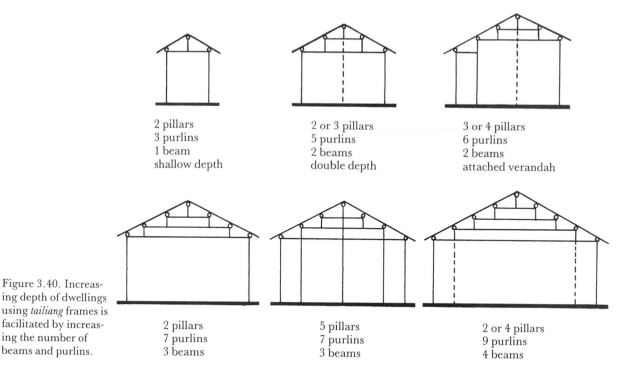

2 pillars
3 purlins
1 beam
shallow depth

2 or 3 pillars
5 purlins
2 beams
double depth

3 or 4 pillars
6 purlins
2 beams
attached verandah

Figure 3.40. Increasing depth of dwellings using *tailiang* frames is facilitated by increasing the number of beams and purlins.

2 pillars
7 purlins
3 beams

5 pillars
7 purlins
3 beams

2 or 4 pillars
9 purlins
4 beams

building space, "borrowing the sky instead of the land" as a Zhejiang folk saying states it (Figure 3.41).

As a general rule, an increase in the depth of a dwelling is reflected in increased height. Extending the depth from a single to a double bay augments the potentially usable space beneath the rafters by a factor of three as seen in Figure 3.42. A building addition may be attached simply by placing a row of pillars to the desired position and interlocking additional transverse tie beams (*chuanfang*). Figure 3.43 shows that even where the terrain is uneven, a stepped dwelling may be built down the slope by utilizing a linked series of pillars and beams without compromising the integrity of the common framing systems. In each of these cases, the framing system at once regulates the two-dimensional area of the resulting *jian* and permits flexibility in the building's overall layout.

Roof Profiles

Aside from flat and shedlike roof profiles, four major types are typical: *yingshanding, xuanshanding, sizhuding* (also called *sihuding*), and *xieshanding*. These four types were well developed two thousand years ago during the Han dynasty and remain today the principal profiles seen in China. All may include either the *tailiang* or *chuandou* framing systems. The profiles are generally symmetrical, although in some larger dwellings a mixture of styles may be found. The Chinese recognized early the significance of eaves (*yanzi*) and gables (*shanqiang*), and it is these elements which help to distinguish the four roof profiles.

The *yingshanding* or "firm mountain" type is common not only with rural dwellings on the north China plain but also in urban courtyard-style houses (*siheyuan*). This type is especially

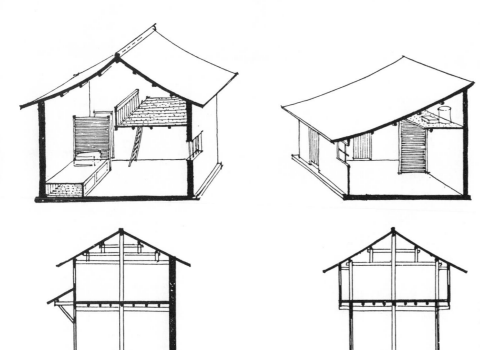

Figure 3.41. With *tailiang* and *chuandou* frames, height is increased by using taller pillars that are tied to floor joists to support lofts or second floors.

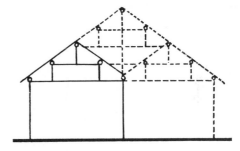

Figure 3.42. Doubling the depth of a dwelling triples the space beneath the rafters and allows room for a loft, a common feature of dwellings in southern China.

suited to areas of limited rainfall where there is no need for overhanging eaves on the gabled end (*shanqiang*) to protect the walls from weathering. In addition to the flush gables characteristic of this type, the eaves on the south-facing facade are foreshortened to enable the low sun of winter to penetrate the dwelling. Typical examples are seen in Figures 3.44 and 3.45, representing modest dwellings in the northeastern and northwestern parts of the country where rainfall is generally less than 750 millimeters. Some *yingshan* gable walls are found in areas of substantial rainfall as in central and southern China. Figure 3.46 shows a rural residential complex near Wuxi in Jiangsu province. Kiln-dried bricks and plaster are used with these walls so that the lack of an overhang on the solid wall is of little environmental significance.

Widely distributed as well, the *xuanshanding* or "overhanging gables" roof offers some protection to the gable walls and is usually accompanied by eaves on the front and back of the dwelling as well. The gable eaves are supported by projecting purlins as seen in Figure 3.47 of an especially common triple-bay dwelling found in Xinglong *xian*, Hebei province. This modest dwelling is

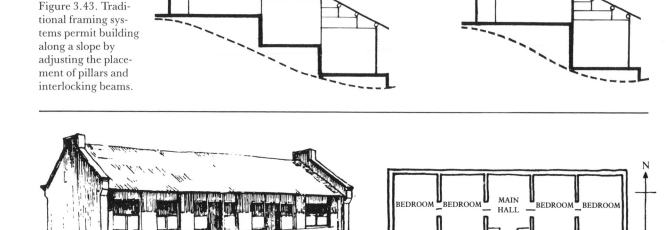

Figure 3.43. Traditional framing systems permit building along a slope by adjusting the placement of pillars and interlocking beams.

Figure 3.44. *Yingshanding* ("firm mountain") roof profile as found in Haerbin in northeastern China.

built on an earthen wall which rests upon a stone base. The depth of the front and back eaves as well as the gable overhang for the *xuanshanding* and also the *sizhuding* and *xieshanding* types, to be discussed next, are often functionally determined but sometimes are specifically emphasized for aesthetic reasons. The extension of the eaves in these cases is accomplished by cantilevered structures that add not only a utilitarian walkway beneath but an apparent lightness to the roof as shown in Figure 3.48 of a dwelling in Sichuan province. Figure 3.49 portrays some of the eaves overhang systems found in a variety of dwellings in Sichuan province.

Both the *sizhuding* and *xieshanding* roof profiles are most common with large residences, temples, and palaces, although they are sometimes found on smaller dwellings. The *sizhuding* or *wudianding* is a hipped roof with four slopes; the *xieshanding* is a variant form combining the *yingshanding* (gabled type) with the *sizhuding* (hipped type). The architectural historian Liu Dunzhen contends that the hipped style was used widely for dwellings prior to the Song dynasty but as a result of sumptuary regulations imposed during the Ming and Qing periods it was restricted subsequently to palace construction as can be seen throughout the Forbidden City in Beijing (Liu Dunzhen 1957, 30). In spite of such restrictions, hipped roofs were placed on some rural dwellings, especially in areas at a distance from imperial control. Figure 3.50 shows a modest dwelling found in Songjiang *xian*, Jiangsu province. The multiple ridge lines of both the *sizhuding* and *xieshanding* styles sometimes take

evolution of the elements and character of *dougong* during the Tang, Song, and Qing periods is well documented for monumental architecture (Han 1973; Qi 1981; Liang 1983; Steinhardt, 1984a). Utilizing a structure which included *dou* (blocks), *gong* (arms), and *ang* (cantilever), *dougong* originally functioned to strengthen the linkage between roof and columns. Increasingly they came principally to serve more decorative purposes. This is as true with great temples and halls as with the larger, more expressive domestic architectural forms. *Dougong* and the accompanying eaves, whether serving functional or aesthetic purposes, highlighted the roof and transformed it into the most significant element of a Chinese building.

Composition of the Roof

Although a roof may be an expressive feature of a building, its principal function is to shelter the

Figure 3.45. *Yingshanding* roof profile of a wall composed of adobe bricks. This brick bonding pattern is widespread throughout China and involves a course of stretchers topped by a course of headers set on edge. South of Xian, Shaanxi province.

a graceful curve, with the curvature accentuated by flying eaves at the ends to form sweeping swallowtail *(yanweixing)* roof profiles (Figure 3.51).

Bracketing systems *(dougong)* have been an important corollary component of many buildings with *sizhuding* or *xieshanding* profiles. To support extended roof eaves, rudimentary bracketing systems emerged as early as the first millennium B.C. and were widespread by the Han dynasty. The

Figure 3.46. Side view of a stepped *yingshanding* roof on a large residence near Wuxi, Jiangsu province.

Figure 3.47. *Xuanshanding* ("overhanging gables") roof profile, Xinglong *xian,* Hebei province.

Figure 3.48. A steep pitch to the roof as well as generous eaves and gable overhang are characteristic of this dwelling in western Sichuan province.

structure and its interior from the elements, especially precipitation. Thus roof construction in areas of significant rain and snow must concern itself with the means to lead the precipitation to the eaves and retard the penetration of moisture.

This end is accomplished generally by sloping the roof and using waterproof materials. In some areas the roof may also have to insulate against cold and heat.

Climate has a preponderant influence on the form of a dwelling. The neolithic dwellings found at Banpo in Shaanxi and at Zhengzhou in Henan reveal the early uses of slope and materials to meet the environmental challenge. (See Figures 1.3 to 1.5.) Roofs with double slopes became canonical elements of Chinese buildings as indicated by representative Chinese pictographs as early as the seventeenth century B.C. Although tiles were in use during the Western Zhou period (1100–771 B.C.), their use in common dwellings was a later development. Chinese peasants, craftsmen, and builders over time developed, generally under conditions of scarcity, a range of materials and compositions to form the roof.

Joseph Spencer noted in the 1940s that "in roofing materials Chinese buildings present a striking example of the relative dominance of two types of material for ordinary use. Half-burnt

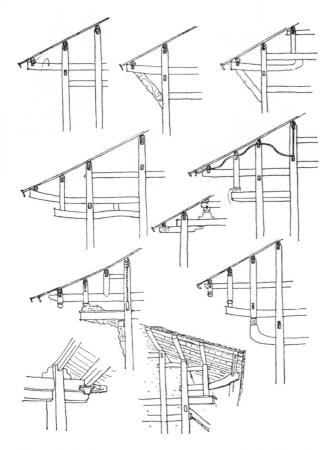

Figure 3.49. Eaves overhang systems in use in dwellings in Sichuan province.

natural chemicals which contribute to water-repellent and insulating properties, the thatching used widely in China could be set directly on the purlins to protect the roof. Buck's research revealed that only in the winter wheat–kaoliang region, which included the Shandong peninsula as well as parts of Hebei, Henan, Anhui, and northern Jiangsu, was thatching more common than other types of roofing. This pattern clearly reflected the poverty of these areas at that time. Elsewhere in the wheat regions of the north, other roofing materials including limited use of tile predominated. Except in the southern double-cropping rice region comprising Guangdong and Guangxi provinces where the use of thatching was negligible, thatch roofs were almost as common as tile roofs throughout the area south of the Yangzi River.

The type of thatching used depended upon local availability. Grasses, reeds, and straw were used extensively all over the country. Throughout north China, thatching has consisted mainly of wheat straw *(maijie)*, kaoliang stalks *(gaoliang gan)*, millet stalks *(xiaomi gan)*, and reeds *(luwei)*. In the early part of the twentieth century in the northeast, one observer noted

gray tile and straw thatch are so common as to seem universal'' (1947, 260). John Lossing Buck's earlier study portrayed strong regional variation in the use of tile and thatching and revealed that other roofing materials were common, especially in northern China, as shown in Table 3.1.

The use of thatch *(maocao)* as roof covering, as shown in Figures 3.52 and 4.8, came early but has endured to the present as a common roofing material on the dwellings of the poor as well as on the rural residences of the literati who sought inspiration from simple rural life. Containing

the building of the thatched millet roofs and the use of kaoliang stems instead of timber. Rafters were set in the usual way and covered with a layer about 2 inches thick of the long kaoliang stems stripped of their leaves and tops. These were tied together and to the rafters with twine thus forming a sort of matting. A layer of thin clay mortar was then spread over the surface and well trowelled until it began to show on the underside. Over this was applied a thatch of small millet stems bound in bundles 8 inches thick, cut square across the butts to 18 inches in length. They were dipped in water and laid in courses after the manner of shingles, but the butts of the stems were driven forward to a slope which obliterated the shoulder, making the courses invisible.

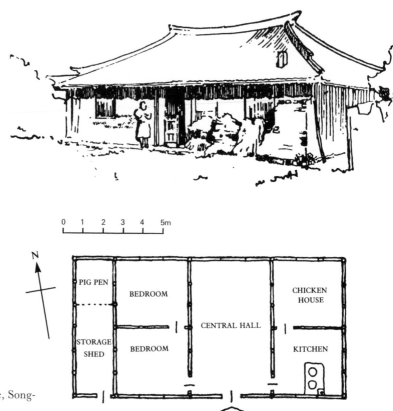

0 1 2 3 4 5m

N

| PIG PEN | BEDROOM | | CHICKEN HOUSE |
| STORAGE SHED | BEDROOM | CENTRAL HALL | KITCHEN |

Figure 3.50. *Sizhuding* or hipped-roof profile, Song-jiang *xian,* Jiangsu province.

Figure 3.51. Details of the eaves and ridge lines of dwellings with a *yanweixing* ("swallowtail") roof profile.

Table 3.1. Roofing Materials of Farm Buildings: 1929–1933

Region	Thatched Roofs	Tile Roofs	Other Materials
China Totals	28%	48%	24%
Wheat region	30%	25%	45%
Rice region	26%	68%	6%
Wheat region			
Spring wheat	0	11%	89%
Winter wheat–millet	7%	55%	38%
Winter wheat–kaoliang	55%	13%	32%
Rice region			
Yangzi rice–wheat	41%	51%	8%
Rice–tea	10%	82%	8%
Sichuan rice	44%	55%	1%
Double-cropping rice	2%	98%	0
Southwestern rice	31%	59%	10%
By size of farm			
Small	36%	39%	25%
Medium	29%	48%	23%
Large	19%	58%	23%

Source: Buck (1937, 443).

Figure 3.52. Small thatched dwelling on the north China plain.

In the better houses this thatching may be plastered with earth mortar or with an earth-lime mortar, which is less liable to wash in heavy rain. [King 1927, 143–144]

Similar procedures are used today, as can be seen in Figure 3.53 of a stone dwelling on the slopes of Taishan in Shandong province. In southern China, rice straw *(daocao)* and wild grasses *(yecao)* have commonly been used to form an impervious thatched roofing.

Buck's investigation showed that even in the early 1930s nearly half the farm buildings throughout the country had tile roofs and more than two-thirds in the rice region. Although there are variations in the shapes and patterns of half-burnt brick *(qinghuiwa)*, the making of roof tiles was similar in the areas investigated by Rudolf Hommel in the 1920s. Local river mud or clay would be worked into a suitable consistency before being molded as a cylinder on a potter's wheel, much as was the practice in the seventeenth century as portrayed in Figure 3.54. Once unmolded and allowed to air dry for a day or so, the cylinders would be broken into four concave segments. The roofs of houses illustrated in this volume clearly show that the placement of tiles and the nature of the surface they might be set upon depends not only on local preference but also available resources. Figure 3.55 summarizes the common tile patterns. The semicircular tiles could be placed in an alternating fashion directly upon roof rafters or roof boards held in place either by their own weight (Figure 3.56) or a mixture of lime and soil to increase the waterproofing quality of the roof (Figure 3.57).

Apart from thatch or tile, other roofing materials are found in north China. In the drier areas of northern Hebei, Shanxi, Shaanxi, the steppes of Inner Mongolia, and in some areas of the

Figure 3.53. The preparation of a thatched roof using a base of kaoliang stalks. Taishan, Shandong province.

Figure 3.54. As shown in a seventeenth-century manual, roof tiles are made on a cylindrical core mold from which four individual tiles can be formed. The same method is used widely today.

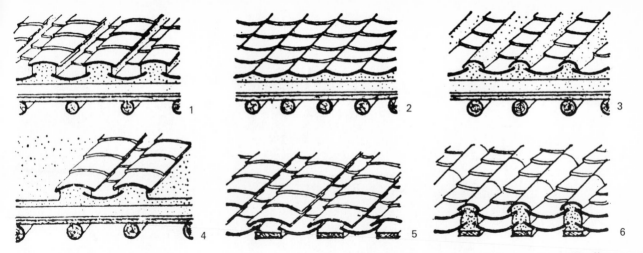

Figure 3.55. Tile patterns used in the construction of rural dwellings: (1) alternating concave and convex pattern; (2) adjacent concave pattern; (3) concave tiles with lime mortar capping pattern; (4) alternating tiles and mortar pattern; (5) southern overlapping and alternating concave and convex pattern; (6) southern double-tile pattern for heat insulation.

Figure 3.56. Gray roof tiles are placed directly on the rafters of this new dwelling in Guangxi Zhuang Autonomous Region.

Figure 3.57. A mixture of lime and mud is spread over the rafters before the roof tiles are added. Taiyuan, Shanxi province.

northeast, roofs that are flat, curved, or slightly pitched with little overhang are common. Many of these roofs are layered compositions of materials of vegetable and mineral origin. The details of the layering vary significantly from place to place.

No comprehensive study has been made of the folk practices used in surfacing a roof. Suggestive of the materials and methods employed are several examples from north and northeastern China. On single-slope, double-slope, and convex roofs, layers would be built up. First roof boards *(wangban)*, a reed mat *(luxi)*, or both would be laid upon the rafters, although in poorer dwellings this layer sometimes would be ignored. Upon this layer either reeds *(luwei)* or kaoliang stalks *(gaoliang gan)* would be spread. The thickness of this vegetable layer differed from place to place. In a cold area, as in Jilin province in the northeast where an insulating layer was important, the layer reached 10 centimeters while in Henan and Hebei provinces it fell in the range of 5 to 6 centimeters.

Two or three layers of a mud and straw composition are placed over the vegetable layer. The basic components are local mud and wheat straw, although in some areas around Beijing hemp is substituted for wheat straw. This composition is tamped down on the roof until it is smooth, and then it is covered with one or two layers of a mixture of lime *(shihui)* and mortar *(qinghui)*. Liu Dunzhen noted three slightly varying methods which are shown in Figure 3.58. In Zhaoxian, Hebei province, three layers are added to the reed matting. First is a 10-centimeter layer of mud. Then comes a mixture of mud, wheat stalks, and lime; tamped down or put under pressure using rocks, this second layer is reduced from a thickness of 10 centimeters to 8 centimeters. The third and final level is a composition of lime and mud in a ratio of 3:7. It too is put under pressure. Crushed coal cinders *(meizha)* may be substituted for mud where they are more readily available. In Jilin province where the layer of wheat-straw mud has a depth of 20 centimeters, the uppermost level

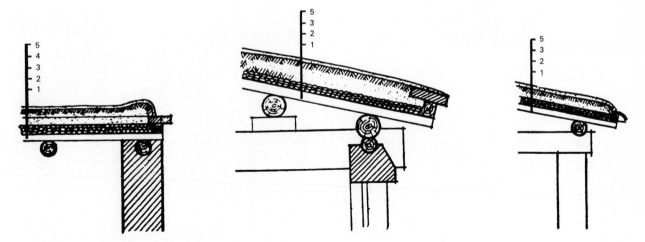

Figure 3.58. The layered composition of roofs in northern China. *Left:* Zhaoxian to the southwest of Beijing. *Center:* Jilin in northeastern China. *Right:* Near Zhengzhou in Henan province. In all three cases, rafters (1) are placed across the purlins and a layer of reeds or kaoliang stalks (2) varying in thickness is added as insulation; the thickest layer is approximately 10 centimeters on the Jilin roof. Atop this layer mud mixed with wheat straw is added in successive layers (3 and 4), each tamped with a wooden rammer. The roof surface (5) is finished with a mixture of lime, ashes, or mud according to local custom.

is a composition comprising alkaline soil. In some cases where such soil is in short supply, alkaline water or saltwater may be added to local mud to form the composition.

The calcination or roasting of limestone and shells to produce lime is an old practice, as evidenced in Figure 3.59, one that recognized that "with calcining or heating, stones can be made to perform wondrous things" (Sung 1966, 201). Not only a waterproofing adhesive in the layered composition roofs of north China, lime serves also as the basic component for plasters that harden after application on walls, floors, and ceilings for mortar and cement and was used as such as early as the Shang and Zhou periods, as indicated in Chapter 1. Depending upon the practice and need in an area, tamped earth, adobe brick, and wattled walls traditionally might be spread with lime or lime-mixture plaster. The resulting white wall surfaces not only are waterproof but also are reflective, an especially suitable combination in

the hot and wetter areas of southern China. The increasing use of fired brick and concrete construction in the country has spurred the production of lime, as has its use in agriculture to reduce soil acidity.

Throughout the country where sedimentary rocks which contain more than fifty percent carbonate materials can be found, there are lime kilns, often side-by-side with kilns for the firing of bricks. Where significant amounts of calcified raw materials are available, large kilns may be built of stone against the slope of a hill. Widely seen today are more temporary kilns, as in Figure 3.60, that continue traditional methods of calcination. Alternating thick layers of coal and roughly cut hunks of limestone within the brick-faced kiln, a hearth is formed with the appearance of an inverted cone with its apex removed. Burning is initiated from the bottom with coal dust or kindling and allowed to continue for about a week until the high temperatures have reduced or crumbled the

灰成石烧饼煤

烧蛎房法

Figure 3.59. The calcination or roasting of limestone and shells is an old practice in China, as depicted in the seventeenth-century *Tiangong kaiwu*.

Figure 3.60. Kilns are found with increasing frequency in rural China today to produce lime for agriculture as well as building purposes. Within the kiln, coal and blocks of limestone are layered before firing.

Figure 3.61. Slate is used as a roof covering on this new two-story complex in northwestern Henan.

stone. After a dousing with water from the top, the kiln is allowed to smolder until it is time to remove the calcined limestone. Using shovels and hoes, the product is pulverized, then screened to eliminate cinders and other coarse materials. Transported to construction sites, the lime is further screened before mixing with mortar, vegetable fiber, or earth for building purposes.

These are but representative methods of forming a waterproof covering for common dwellings (Liu Dunzhen 1957, 27–29). As the field information collected by Buck indicates (Table 3.1), these methods are most prevalent in the northern areas of the country where tile and thatch roofs are not common. In fact, the methods are used widely in these areas even at the present time. Where locally available, slate is employed as a roof covering on small houses as well as on modern two-story dwellings like the ones shown in Figure 3.61.

SUMMARY

Chinese rural construction over the years has derived largely from experience rather than theory, and expresses frugality and often poverty rather than ostentation and wealth. The standardization of the *jian* or bay as the basic modular unit of building enforced a discipline on rectangular dwellings. With an order of measure and layout, Chinese peasants nonetheless built with an indifference to permanence using earth and wood as their principal materials. With entry usually on the long side, the facade and roof of the house became linked structurally and visually as the most pronounced element. Chinese houses often separate the elements of support from those of enclosure as in the orthodox building tradition for important buildings, yet one is more likely to find load-bearing walls in a rural dwelling than in a more substantial building such as a palace or temple. Acutely conscious of the natural environment, Chinese peasants adapted the basic rectangular design to a variety of environmental conditions. Low houses in the north prove suitable for warmth in winter while high ones in the south ensure summer ventilation. Often without back rooms and frequently oriented so that front rooms receive the sun, the typical Chinese rural dwelling turned its back to the severe winds of winter.

CHAPTER 4

The Rural Dwelling on China's Taiwan Frontier

THE colonization of Taiwan by the Chinese was essentially a process that lasted two centuries. Chinese migration, beginning in the second quarter of the seventeenth century, brought several thousand destitute peasants from the Zhangzhou and Quanzhou areas of Fujian to the southwest coastal plain of the island where they encountered aboriginal tribes. Such movements were spurred by the Dutch occupation and then by the subsequent control of the island by the forces of the Ming loyalist Zheng Chenggong. Beginning in 1624, the Dutch established relative order and provided draft oxen, farm implements, and seeds to those Chinese willing to open up the wilderness. The movement was facilitated by the unsettled conditions in China which presaged the changing of dynasty from the Ming to the alien Qing (Manchu). By about 1650, some 25,000 Chinese male settlers were recorded in the Dutch areas. The tempo of migration increased after 1661 when Zheng Chenggong, the celebrated Koxinga, expelled the Dutch from the island. By the time military forces of the Qing dynasty defeated Zheng's descendants in 1683, the Chinese population had reached perhaps 350,000.

Erratic and clandestine movements of people across the straits put stress on the concentrated areas of Chinese settlement in the southwest and provided the catalyst which pushed Chinese settlement not only northward but, after a time, also into the longitudinal rift valley of the east coast. By 1887 Taiwan had as many as 3 million Chinese settlers. During this period, Chinese peasant pioneers confronted the raw frontier and its aboriginal inhabitants and transformed the grasslands and forests into tributary communities that increasingly came to resemble the cultural hearths on the mainland (Hsu 1980; Knapp 1976).

Chinese pioneers in Taiwan throughout the period from the seventeenth to the twentieth century came almost exclusively from the contiguous provinces of Fujian and Guangdong which lay opposite the island. Although sharing a common Han cultural heritage, pronounced subethnic distinctions among them contributed to a variety of cultural responses in Taiwan. The southeastern coastal area of China had distinct and diverse subcultures to a degree not equaled elsewhere in China. Often isolated by rugged topography, mainland peasant communities in this region were further divided by significant linguistic differences and lineage patterns which together reinforced cultural involution. Those from Fujian came principally from the Quanzhou and Zhangzhou areas and spoke varieties of the Southern Min (Minnan) dialect, linguistic variations which were to some extent mutually unintelligible. Migrants from Guangdong were largely Hakka (Kejia), known for their clannishness, who spoke several further subdialects (Lamley 1981, 283–296). Migrants to the island generally did not blend with one another, but instead separated according to the townships and villages from which they had originated. A Japanese survey of 1926 illustrated for even that late date the exclusiveness of settlement patterns in Taiwan (Governor-General 1928).

Early Dwellings and Family Organization

Seventeenth and eighteenth-century pioneers undoubtedly brought with them to Taiwan images of rural dwellings that would have been appropriate on the island. No full-form Chinese dwellings were built during the early years of residence, however, largely because of a reluctance to recognize the island as domicile. The recreation of these early dwellings is fraught with difficulty. No document details the construction and layout of structures as simple and ubiquitous as the peasant abode. Like Western chroniclers, the authors of Chinese gazetteers of the period chose instead to elaborate on the exotic elements of "native" (that is, aboriginal) life, including, in at least one case, the raising of a thatched roof on an aboriginal dwelling (Zhou 1717, 21).

Early arrivals were often single males who saw themselves as sojourners, quasi-transients, adrift until they either returned to their home villages or secured a firm foothold on Taiwan with the creation of a nuclear family. Chinese texts give prominence to the unbalanced male/female ratios, a condition fostered by rugged frontier life, dangers in crossing the straits, and Qing dynasty policies before 1790 which forbade the migration of women (Dai 1963, 58; Zhuang 1964, 50). Qing policies, moreover, initially made it impossible for the migration of groups who shared a lineage relationship. Consequently many of the migrants were poor mainland peasants out to seek a fortune on the island and then "return to one's home village in silken robes" (yijin huanxiang). When they were successful, chain migration resulted as other single males were induced to move by earlier arrivals. In some cases, land reclamation was undertaken by entrepreneurs who acquired patents (kenzhao) and invited former soldiers to carry out the work (Knapp 1980, 60–64).

For these settlers in the seventeenth century, the domicile housing the ancestral tablets which signified family succession and continuity remained in the mainland ancestral home area to be visited periodically to discharge filial obligations. Mere shelter, rather than a substitute base for ancestral paraphernalia, met the needs of most of the peasant pioneers. Simple dwellings erected of bamboo, reed, or grass matting, perhaps after the manner of the plains aborigines, most likely were common. Sketchy pictorial representations in eighteenth and nineteenth-century difang zhi (gazetteers), such as the one shown in Figure 4.1, only begin to suggest the common houses of early settlers. Further limited evidence is to be found in the large number of settlement names which incorporate liao, cuo, wo, and wu—characters that imply dwellings of humble appearance and simple construction for which the English equivalents "hut," "shack," or at most "cottage" would be appropriate.

The clearing of wilderness land, its reclamation, and the accumulation of wealth were not a

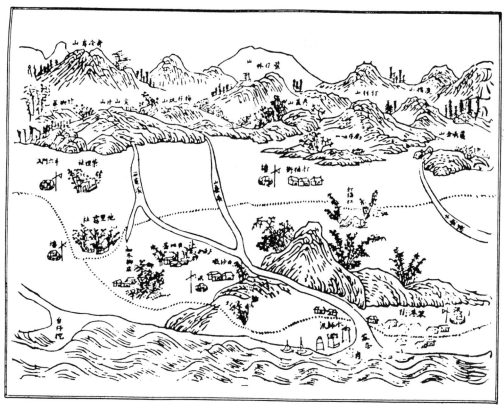

Figure 4.1. This representation from the 1717 *Zhulo xian zhi* (Zhulo *xian* gazetteer) contrasts Chinese and aboriginal dwellings on Taiwan's western coastal plain. The dwellings found in the aboriginal villages *(she)* are raised on piles and covered with thatching. The Chinese dwellings are set directly on the ground and all appear to be oriented south or southwest.

hurried process on the Taiwan frontier. Rural economic development through the improvement of land and the extension of water conservancy was the precondition for transition from groupings of unrelated males to a more stable and permanent community resting on the social base of Chinese society: the family. In the absence of women, some peasant males, perhaps forty or fifty years of age who had decided to stay on Taiwan, adopted young boys to be raised as legal sons in order to provide for succession in the ceremonial as well as proprietary sense. On the Taiwan frontier, such adoption went beyond the sons of younger or older brothers; even sons with different surnames might be adopted.

These new relationships transformed even a humble dwelling from simple shelter to new societal purposes. Furthermore, the sexual imbalance began to tilt in time as males married sinicized aboriginal women or were able to obtain wives from their home community. With the formation of the conjugal unit and the attenuation of links with mainland villages, as well as the accumulation of sufficient resources, more substantial and permanent rural dwellings were necessarily built. For the most part, such dwellings were built with the peasants' own hands using available materials and adhered to, but were not limited by, customary practices.

A dwelling is more than a vessel for daily life. It

is a dynamic entity that expresses in varying degrees the organization, fortunes, aspirations, and status of those living within it. Family *(jia)* organization on the Taiwan frontier emerged with the formation of a conjugal unit within a simple rectangular dwelling with the *jia* serving as the basic unit of production and consumption. Changes in the size and composition of the *jia,* according to expectations, would bring it through a cycle of development from the nuclear or elementary form to the stem form and eventually perhaps the joint form before division *(fenjia)* would restart the cycle (Cohen 1970 and 1976). Empirical studies have shown that internal as well as external forces operate on the Chinese family and guide its passage from one organizational form to another.

The anthropological literature on Taiwan reveals an extraordinary flexibility regarding the family as basic domestic institution. As summarized by Arthur Wolf (1981, 343):

Differences in family size and complexity cannot be explained with reference to rules, norms, or ideals. Basically, the Chinese family is the same everywhere; all that varies are the conditions that make large families more or less advantageous. If the families of the wealthy are larger than those of the poor, this is not because they are governed by different ideals. It is only because wealth encourages diversification and thereby makes cooperation mutually advantageous.

Thus in some areas of the island small households remained the norm, as married sons set up separate households where it was economically advantageous to do so. This pattern was especially true in coastal fishing villages while larger households were characteristic of more economically advanced and diversified areas (Wang 1971). Since household size obviously manifested itself in the size of the dwelling, there was a diversity of dwelling patterns at any given time.

ORTHODOX PATTERNS OF SHAPE AND SIZE

Mainland practices and patterns, emphasizing symmetry, axiality, and balance, guided the shape, size, and orientation of early dwellings on the island. Sumptuary regulations, inherited from the Ming period by the Qing, were applicable to Taiwan but were frequently ignored. During the early stages of family formation, a solitary structure of a single story *(pingfang)* with either of two floor plans was prevalent. The simplest was a rectangular room which served as common room as well as for sleeping. The second plan derived from the erection of partitions on either side of the central section or main hall *(gongting, zhengting,* or *keting).* Balance and symmetry were maintained by having the rooms total odd numbers, usually one or three, and placing a door in the center of the front wall. Axiality was represented by the long side of the rectangle, an alignment tied to the expression of significance and seniority.

The *gongting* of even a basic unit served ritual as well as secular purposes. Symbolic of continuity and facing the door, the main hall commonly contained a high, long table upon which were arranged in an orthodox order ancestral tablets, images of gods and goddesses, as well as the paraphernalia of ceremony. Ancestors were placed on stage right and the gods on stage left, the position of higher rank. On the wall behind, a large portrait of a deity and a pair of couplets *(duilian)* were hung. Periodic offerings of food and incense related to prescribed ritual underscored the centrality of the room in acknowledging patrilineal descent and communal links. Usually the room was high, and its exposed beams were invariably blackened by the recurring smoke from incense placed in a burner hung near the entrance. The room opened to the outside through double-leafed doors which brought the only light inside. To this room, male members of the family who were near death would be brought as an expression of articulation within the descent group. This *gongting* remained joint property never to be divided even if other components of the developed compound estate were portioned out.

To the left and right of the altar-bearing *gongting,* balanced rooms served as sleeping quarters or other functional needs. The total number of rooms summed to three, five, or later seven: "Odd is 'good' because it creates symmetry; even is 'bad' because it results in asymmetry" (Wang 1974, 183). The sleeping room to stage left of the altar-bearing hall was reserved for parents and termed *dafang* ("great room"). When the eldest son married, the parents might vacate the room and take another, usually the *erfang* ("second room") located on the opposite side of the central hall. Such an ordering recognized significance and seniority in much the same way as the placement of deities and tablets on the ancestral table itself. Ultimately, the number and gender of children as well as the family's fortunes determined the number of sleeping rooms and the degree of necessary rotation, but it was the distance from the center and the left/right location which guided the changes. Movement along the axis away from the *gongting* was a passage from public space to private domain in much the same way that it was in the more fully developed courtyard house which had its depth along a longitudinal axis.

This linear core building served as the nucleus from which ramified structures could be attached to accommodate the growing family and proclaim its aspirations. Anticipated expansion from the rectangular base might be suggested by an unnecessary door or a bricked-in passageway, as shown in Figure 4.2, to be opened as necessity dictated.

Orthodox additions would be arranged perpendicularly to the axis of the core rectangle. These connecting side buildings, termed *xiangfang* on the mainland, were called *hulong* ("protector dragons") in Taiwan. They served subsidiary purposes, such as bedrooms for younger members of the family, storage, or cooking space. Erected first to stage left and then to stage right, these wings had accordant rooflines somewhat lower than the main body *(zhengshen)* of the dwelling. Embraced between the wings was the courtyard, which symbolically focused the family spirit *(qi).* In northern Taiwan, the courtyard traditionally was left open as shown in Figure 4.3. With dwellings in southern Taiwan, shown in Figure 4.4, the unity of the three-sided compound *(sanheyuan)* was sometimes completed with the addition of a waist-high wall. In both cases, the courtyard served as access path

Figure 4.2. This bricked-in passageway of a contemporary rectangular core building anticipates the addition of a *hulong* or wing to the body of the dwelling.

Figure 4.3. On the right is a *hulong* or wing with rooflines of decreasing heights. The opposite *hulong* and central body of the house embrace a courtyard *(chen)* for drying grain. The complex is fronted by a pond, dug to provide earth for the foundation of the house as well as for geomantic reasons. Taoyuan *xian,* northern Taiwan.

from and to each component of the dwelling, provided space for carrying out household chores outside the dark interiors, and served as drying floor for agricultural products.

Guided by idealized family norms, the conjugal unit could evolve to stem and joint forms through the marriage of sons. As wealth and human relationships allowed, this evolution sometimes led to a restructuring of domestic space beyond the U shape. Growth would be either in a lateral or a forward direction, depending on the socioeconomic circumstances of the household. Farm households normally grew laterally; the domiciles

of ambitious gentry stretched to greater depth. Additional wings, usually as pairs, could be placed parallel to the basic wings *(hulong)* and duplicated when necessary. The initial or inner pair was termed *neihu* ("inner protectors"), the second *waihu* ("outer protectors"), and the next *waiwaihu* ("outer outer protectors"). One well-developed residence in Xinpu, east of the city of Xinzhu, had six pairs of *hulong.*

Figure 4.5 shows the Antai Lin residence in Taibei, a fine example of lateral expansion revealing a central courtyard pattern *(siheyuan)* with two pair of *hulong* (Lee 1977, 20). Built at the end of

Figure 4.4. Open-courtyard dwelling in southern Taiwan, near Tainan, with a low wall completing the *sanheyuan*.

Figure 4.5. The An Tai Lin residence in eastern Taibei with a double pair of *hulong,* both *neihu* and *waihu,* and an internal courtyard.

the eighteenth or beginning of the nineteenth century, it is representative of residences built following the traditional style of southern Fujian province on the mainland. Lin Zhineng, for whom it was built, was a well-to-do merchant who sited his dwelling among the rice fields of the eastern Taibei basin and built it using stone, wood, and tiles brought to Taiwan as ballast in his cargo ships. The building was dismantled in 1978 and has now been rebuilt in a park in northern Taibei.

In addition to lateral growth, large rural residences on the island were sometimes designed to stretch with greater depth from the main entrance. A grand example of this type is the Lin family manse located in Banqiao, in the southwest corner of the Taibei basin. In this dwelling, built in three main parts during the nineteenth century, a hierarchy of privacy evolved as the fortunes of the Lin family developed. This graduated privacy evolved from an original courtyard-style dwelling which was built in 1847 using the classic *siheyuan* pattern with a three-unit (*jian*) core building, two wings (*hulong*), and a gate. An adjacent three-courtyard residence was built in 1853 by two sons. The son of one of these men began in 1888 an even larger five-courtyard residence together with an elaborate garden; the project was completed in 1893, just two years before the island was occupied by the Japanese (Han and Hong 1973). Having suffered much deterioration over the years, the complex is now undergoing thorough restoration.

In Pingdong county of southern Taiwan there is a residence of great depth which has been maintained relatively intact as a common estate and a symbol of the Xiao family's inseparability. At one time the dwelling housed more than one hundred people but now only a fraction of that number lives there. Composed of five main halls (*jin*) which recede from the entrance, four of which

were constructed more than a century ago and a fifth in the early twentieth century, the building was patterned after the family's Mei county ancestral home in Guangdong province (Figure 4.6). As one progresses from the first hall to the interior, the height of the roofs increases. As a rhythmic counterpoint, the courtyards decrease in size as one moves from outermost hall to the innermost. Within these complex dwellings, internal circulation often was difficult although access to the outside was fairly straightforward.

The smooth progression of a dwelling's growth and expansion suggested here was not always realized. Tensions within the Chinese family had an impact upon the use of residential space:

At some point the family would divide into smaller units, but there might be no change in the compound's residential arrangement other than the construction of additional kitchens. Except for the central room, all rooms in the compound are distributed among the new families during division, together with other such family property as land, farming equipment, or shops. Because the central room is not involved, the first family partition creates two or more families owning in common this room if nothing else. Thus in most compounds there eventually is a multifamily agnatic (patrilineal) group, which continues to increase in its individual membership and in the number of constituent families. At any given time . . . there are compounds (and agnatic groups) at different stages of development; only the base of the U is completed in some compounds, others may already have the full U shape and even two or more wings [Cohen 1976, 21–22]

In an asymmetrically large farmhouse in Shilin, north of Taibei, where more than 150 people lived, the fragmentation of the complex indicates the presence of numerous related nuclear families, preparing food at separate stoves but living within a joint dwelling (Dillingham and Dilling-

Figure 4.6. Receding halls and courtyards as well as abutting side buildings. Xiao family residence, Pingdong *xian,* southern Taiwan.

ham 1971, 60–65, 127). Within this laterally expanded form, the spatial focus remained the central *gongting,* the symbol of the larger family, which together with the first pair of *hulong* and the entrance gate embraced the only true courtyard. The separate stoves reveal that the family had undergone division probably at the time of the father's death or perhaps earlier with the marriages of brothers who did not wish to maintain a joint household. Side-to-side circulation in this compound was routed either along the walkway immediately in front of the central hall or by way of a circuitous route through various rooms; when relations among the residents remained cordial, these rooms served as corridors as well as activity space. Doors, found on most walls, were sometimes nailed shut to underscore the rupture in the family. The layout, however dysfunctional it may

appear in terms of circulation, symbolically declared a degree of unity and status.

Orthodox sizes and shapes express both the functional and the symbolic qualities of the Chinese homestead. Built with an eye to the future, the dwelling suggests more than lifetime occupancy and binds a family to a locale. The relationship among constituent elements of the layout reveals not only a potential for expansion but also the latent likelihood of retrenchment to meet the consequences of family conflict or changes in fortune. The compact shape of the residential ensemble represents an economizing of space. Building freestanding additions to accommodate the needs of collateral relatives is certainly more wasteful of land and other resources than joining new rooms to old ones to form a tight ramified structure. With life carried on inside and outside the dwelling, open spaces gained functional utility and could be enclosed by low walls or surrounding structures to separate them from the world outside. At any given time, the fact that so many rural dwellings remain a single rectangle—without a perpendicular wing or two—suggests the frequent frustration of peasant desires for the accumulation of wealth.

ORIENTATION

As in many areas of the mainland, the selection of building sites and the orientation of dwellings on Taiwan has been guided by the popular yet esoteric set of practices known as *fengshui* (Guan 1980, 184–189; Knapp 1982a, 8–10). *Fengshui*, literally "wind and water" and sometimes called geomancy, encompasses an array of elements that purportedly facilitate the integration of humanity and nature, a topic treated in greater detail in the next chapter.

An examination of rural dwellings in many areas of Taiwan reveals orientations toward the south, east, and west, but rarely does one find a north-facing orientation. Orthodox *fengshui* and canonical orientation as formalized in northern China led to a southern orientation (*zuobei chaonan*). This positioning was altered in southeastern China and carried over to Taiwan, most likely in recognition of the benefit of the winds which blew off the adjoining water in spring and summer. Furthermore, the choice of an optimal site for a dwelling on Taiwan was usually discerned from a consideration of topographical shapes and relationships as well as the directional component just as in many areas of the mainland. One finds many rural dwellings on the island crouching amid the foothills with an embracing hill or ridge to its back. For optimal *fengshui*, a stream was expected to pass some distance from the front gate. In many areas of Taiwan, and particularly on the Taoyuan plain, a pond was dug in front of the dwelling if a free-flowing stream was absent (Figure 4.3).

STRUCTURAL PARTS

The Chinese house, of course, is as much artifact as it is mentifact. Sociocultural forces guide the shape, size, orientation, and layout of the dwelling and may play a role in matters relating to its construction. Yet in giving shape to space, builders in Taiwan molded materials to surround space and to span it. Rural dwellings in Taiwan historically have been single-storied (*pingfang*) until recent decades when the two-storied *loufang* or *yangfang* ("foreign styled") rural residence began to appear.

Foundations and Floors

Along the western lowlands of Taiwan, builders were always conscious of areas of seasonal flooding. Their response, however, was not to elevate a house as in Southeast Asia or Japan but to place the dwelling upon a thoroughly packed raised foundation. Such a foundation was usually several meters larger than the structure itself in order to provide a walkway under the eaves once the house was completed. Dirt was usually hauled in or excavated from a future pond in front of the construction site to raise the level of a low area. Stones, freely available from Taiwan's rubble-strewn streams, commonly have been used to line the top of gravel-packed footings and to serve as the base for the walls. The height of this stone foundation depended on the possibility of flooding. In areas close to rivers, a stone platform sometimes was built to raise the dwelling above flood level, as for the dwelling shown in Figure 4.7.

Figure 4.7. Stones from a nearby stream are used to build a platform in order to raise this bamboo and thatch dwelling above flood level.

Just as with buildings dating back to Shang times, the level ground within the foundation was firmly packed with earth to become the floor. Brick, cement, or ceramic floors were rare except in the houses of the wealthy where the brick would have been brought by ship from the mainland. Indeed, as recently as 1952, in a study of 857 farm households across the island, nearly ninety percent still had dirt floors (Raper 1953, 130). A similar survey in 1958 showed close to eighty percent of 977 households with dirt floors (Kirby 1960, 150). As economic conditions improved on the island throughout the 1960s and 1970s, most floors have been improved with locally made red brick or more recently terrazzo.

Structural Framework

An orthodox characteristic of traditional Chinese architecture is the use of a wooden framework to support the roof. Generally, as discussed in Chapter 3, the walls in such a building are not load-bearing; they serve principally to enclose or screen. A framework of this type has been an integral architectural characteristic of temples, official buildings, and some dwellings on Taiwan. Large

numbers of houses on the island, however, were built without a wooden framework and depend on their adobe or brick walls as structural support for the roof.

Early dwellings used bamboo for pillars and beams just as timber was generally used throughout the mainland, as seen in Figure 4.7. At least six varieties of bamboo were available to meet building needs. The *Zhulo xian zhi* ("Zhulo *xian* Gazetteer") mentions the suitability of *cizhu* (thorny bamboo), which attains a length of 13 to 16 meters, for ridgepoles and pillars. Other types of bamboo, such as the *konghanzhu* variety, grew over 2 meters in length and were used for framing (Zhou 1717, 117). Together with bamboo utilized as struts and laths, the pillars and beams could be joined together easily by tying with rattan *(teng)*. Such structures (Figure 4.8) did not differ much from those of the aborigines. They could be easily built with the pioneer's own hands and proved resilient to wind and earthquake movements (Zhongguo wenhua xueyuan 1974, 37–38). The makeup of the enclosing curtain walls is discussed in the next section.

Wooden frameworks are most conspicuous in

larger dwellings. Both the *tailiang* (pillar and beam) system and the *chuandou* (pillar and transverse tie beam) system have been used on the island. It may be recalled that the *tailiang* system has beams resting on anterior and posterior pillars (Figure 3.36). Upon each beam two struts rise to support a shorter beam. Successive tiers of beams rising in this way define the pitch of the roof. At the juncture of a pillar and a beam, a purlin is laid to support the roof rafters. The *chuandou* system differs from the *tailiang* system in that transverse tie beams *(chuan)* are tenoned into the pillars to create a framework (Figure 3.36). Moreover, in the *chuandou* frame the purlins are set directly on the pillars which reach increasing heights in defining the profile of the roof.

No nails are used in either system. It is the composition of the pillars and beams as well as the weight of the rising framework which ensures the system's integrity. Used instead of a truss to determine the pitch of the roof, this repertoire of pillars and beams provides structural flexibility as well as freedom in fixing the curvature of the roof—a distinctive characteristic of the architectural tradition of Taiwan and the southeast coast of the mainland. As in the simple bamboo frameworks mentioned above, the walls did not carry the weight of the roof and were mere curtain walls. Swaying movements due to earthquakes could be damped progressively without danger in buildings utilizing the *tailiang* or *chuandou* frameworks.

Many adobe and brick structures on the island,

Figure 4.8. A twentieth-century bamboo framed dwelling with thatched roof. Tile has been used on the addition. Tuku, Zhanghua *xian*.

Figure 4.9. The curtain walls are being raised first for this dwelling on the outskirts of eastern Taibei, leaving the steel reinforcing rods protruding. In time these rods will be encased as pillars with cement to support the roof.

however, did not have wooden frameworks. Instead, the roofs were supported directly by purlins placed upon indentations in the upper gable ends of the dwelling. This structural type was found on the mainland as well in drier areas where the roof was flat or where wood was costly. During the past twenty years, pillars made of concrete reinforced with steel rods have taken the place of wooden pillars in some home construction (Figure 4.9).

Where pillars supported beams or purlins, their placement defined the common areas known as *jian,* or bays, the basic unit of space in Chinese buildings whether a humble dwelling, a temple, or a ceremonial palace. As a common denominator for Chinese architecture, *jian* have come to represent a flexible modular unit for the division of space and its utilization. This division is usu-

ally apparent from within the Taiwanese house because the ceilings are generally left exposed.

Walls

Early dwellings drew upon the abundant bamboo and other grasses for relatively easy construction. Using bamboo or wood as struts and laths to support the walls, rice straw or rush thatches were tied with pliant rattan to form a peaked roof. Although resilient to the frequent earthquakes on the island and relatively easy to repair, bamboo dwellings had a fairly short life and had to be replaced within twenty years. Father deMailla, a French missionary, reported in 1715 that even in the capital "the houses are covered with straw, and built for the most part of earth and bamboo" (Campbell 1903, 507). Foreign travelers throughout the nineteenth century regularly commented on the dwellings of bamboo thatched with grasses set among the rice fields. (See Swinhoe 1859, 153; Thomson 1873, 100; Beazeley 1885, 7.) Bamboo exceeded all other walling material of rural dwellings even in the middle of the twentieth century (Raper 1953, 125; Kirby 1960, 149). Figure 4.10 shows a mid-twentieth century bamboo-plaited building, covered with mud plaster, not unlike those found in earlier centuries on the island. The figure also shows a more substantial saddleback-roofed dwelling with a colonnaded portico.

Along the northeast coast and on the island of Penghu, coral and stones found along the beach have been used as walling (Figure 4.11). The tamped or pounded earth method of wall construction *(hangtu)* apparently was practiced in Taiwan, although note of it in the records is rare (Chen 1968, 324). Major shortcomings of piled stone and tamped earth no doubt were their susceptibility to earthquake damage and, in the case of tamped earth, the fact that it weathered badly under the copious rainfall of the subtropics.

Sun-dried bricks, as in most areas of China,

Figure 4.10. Bamboo-plaited walls covered with mud plaster are used in the building on the left. The core dwelling with a roof of tile set upon bamboo rafters has overhanging eaves supported by stone columns to form a portico. Zhanghua *xian*.

Figure 4.11. In villages along the northeastern coast of Taiwan, stone is sometimes used for housebuilding. Thatching covers the roof.

have been common construction materials. As on the mainland, bricks were cut from the mud accumulated on the floor of paddy fields, stacked in rows covered by straw, and left to dry for several weeks. Clay could also be dug from a pit at the front of a dwelling, taken from hillsides or the river's edge, mixed with rice straw or rice chaff for strengthening, molded and cut, and then left to dry in the sun for three or four days. Bricks *(tujiao* or *tupi)* took a variety of forms but were commonly 35 or 36 centimeters long, 21 or 22 centimeters wide, and 10 centimeters thick (Chen 1960, 119). Mud brick walls in Taiwan usually supported the roof beams directly without vertical support poles *(zhu)* in the walls. To reduce the premature rotting of roof timbers or bamboo because of contact with the water-absorbent earthen walls, several courses of kiln-dried brick or stone were usually laid on top of the wall.

In the past, a variety of means were used to lessen the weathering of the adobe walls from sub-tropical downpours and the wind. These devices included broad eaves on the front and back of the house but not typically on the ends. Plaited grasses as well as a plaster composed of a mixture of mud and rice chaff *(cukangtu)* were sometimes added to the friable walls to protect them (Kokubu and Shioji 1954, 167–169). In some cases, tile or thin brick veneers were added at the time of initial construction. In others, such embellishment was added piecemeal as a reflection of acquired wealth. Fish-scale shaped tiles arranged like shingles may be seen on some well-maintained older dwellings in the south (Figure 4.12). Throughout the island one sees thin square or rectangular tiles on old houses, each attached to the wall by a spike through its center. It has been claimed that the method was introduced to the island by the Dutch in the seventeenth century (Lin 1975, 24, 26).

Kiln-dried brick houses have existed on Taiwan since the late seventeenth century and, although not common in the nineteenth century, were found in many places. By 1952 only some ten percent of farm households surveyed were of kiln brick construction. Reflecting the rapid development of the island, this proportion reached twenty-five percent in 1958 (Kirby 1960, 149). In some cases, prosperity was evidenced by the replacement of adobe by kiln brick one wall at a time over a period of years. Today kiln brick farmhouses are ubiquitous. Virtually all the large rural dwellings remaining from the nineteenth century are themselves of red kiln brick construction. Government buildings, temples, and the urban dwellings of merchants even in the later part of the seventeenth century were usually built of kiln-dried bricks, called *niaozhuan* ("bird bricks"). These bricks, however, were not normally made in Taiwan but were carried from across the straits. Gray bricks *(huizhuan)* from northern Fujian and red bricks *(hongzhuan)* from the Xiamen area of southern Fujian were carried as ballast on return voyages to the island (Lin 1960, 39).

Figure 4.12. Fish-scale shingles attached to the upper exterior gable walls.

Roofs

A high point of domestic architecture is the roof, whether it is viewed from the perspective of construction materials, shape, or symbolism. Those found on the rural dwellings of Taiwan are clearly derived from those found in southern Fujian. (See Figures 2.31 and 2.33.) All early dwellings and even many public buildings on Taiwan at the time of the Qing takeover in 1683 had thatched roofs of wild grasses *(maocao)* or rice straw. By the end of the seventeenth century, however, tiled roofs began to outnumber thatched roofs in the several major towns on the southwestern coast although thatched roofs were found throughout the rural areas *(Taiwanfu zhi* 1761, 132–136).

Thatched roofs had certain advantages over tiled roofs. Certainly the weight and brittleness of tile roofs were demonstrated during the earthquake of 1792 when more than 20,000 tiled houses and only 1,000 thatched dwellings collapsed (Hsu 1975, 357). These patterns continued well into the 1920s. Although some roof improvements occurred during the 1930s, no significant qualitative changes in rural housing took place. The Joint Commission on Rural Reconstruction found forty-five percent of the rural dwellings surveyed in 1952 still had thatch roofs. This proportion dropped dramatically to twenty percent only six years later—an immediate consequence of the well-known Land-to-the-Tiller program (Kirby 1960, 149). The roof tiles on Taiwan houses take one of two forms. The first, called *hongwa* or red tiles, are slightly arcuate tiles that form ridges down the slope of the roof; they are the most common type used today. *Tongwa* are tiles which give the appearance of sections of bamboo laid end to end. Capped with eaves tiles *(dangwa),* they mimic temples and official buildings.

The roof profile may be viewed from a combination of two perspectives. The first emphasizes the line of the ridgepole *(wuji);* and the other concentrates on the point where the roof meets the gable end of the building. Figures 4.4 and 4.5 portray the slight curvature of the ridge lines of the two most common types found on the island: the *mabeixing* (horseback or saddle) style and the *yanweixing* (swallowtail) style. The so-called horseback pattern dominates roof profiles on Taiwan. With a fairly steep slope, it is suitable for moving rainwater from either a cover of thatch or tiles. The upsweeping curvature of the *yanwei* (swallowtail) was modified from the *chiwei* (owl's tail) used on important traditional Chinese buildings in the northern capitals of the mainland and was officially restricted by sumptuary laws on Taiwan for use only in the construction of temples, official buildings, and the residences of degree holders. The *nouveau riche* on the Taiwan frontier sometimes flouted the law, however, and erected dwellings with the graceful swallowtail roof. This profile was more common in northern Taiwan where enforcement of regulations was less strict. Hipped roofs *(sizhuding* or *wudianding)* were not used for houses in Taiwan.

With the pitch of the roof governed by the system of pillars and beams, the actual slope and curve can be adjusted by altering the spacing ratio

between the beams and struts which support the purlins (Figure 4.13). The greater the distance between beams and struts, the more gentle the pitch of the roof. For some large dwellings and temples, early builders on the island sought greater flexibility in roof design in order to create the appearance of a lighter and more buoyant roof. This effect was accomplished by raising a secondary ridgepole horizontally to the principal ridgepole and placing common rafters according to the new requirements. If well designed, this double roof provided a space through which airflow could carry away the absorbed heat of the sun (Lu 1978, 40–41). Despite this rational consideration, builders commonly filled the open space between the added roof and the interior roof with mud, tile pieces, or bricks. Although increasing the possibility of damage from earthquakes, the dead weight of such roofs offset the force of typhoon winds while giving the appearance of weightlessness.

Most dwellings in Taiwan possess *yingshanding* ("firm mountain") flush gables, although some houses do have roofs with a limited overhang at the gable end. Decorative and stylistic embellishments have been added not only to the upper gables but also to the ridge line above as seen in Figures 4.14 and 4.15. Figure 4.16 further pre-

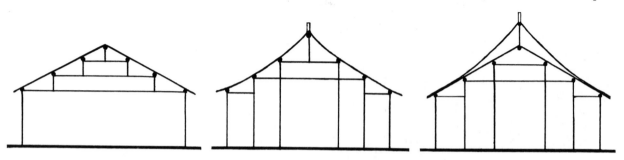

Figure 4.13. By gradually increasing the height of the pillars or posts above the horizontal beams, curvature can be emphasized, as can be seen by comparing the left-hand and center drawings. The right-hand drawing indicates a similar effect that is accomplished by raising a false roof above the normal interior frame.

Figure 4.14. *Mabeixing* ("horseback" or "saddle") roof profile, northern Taiwan.

Figure 4.15. *Yanwei-xing* ("swallowtail") roof profile, Taibei basin.

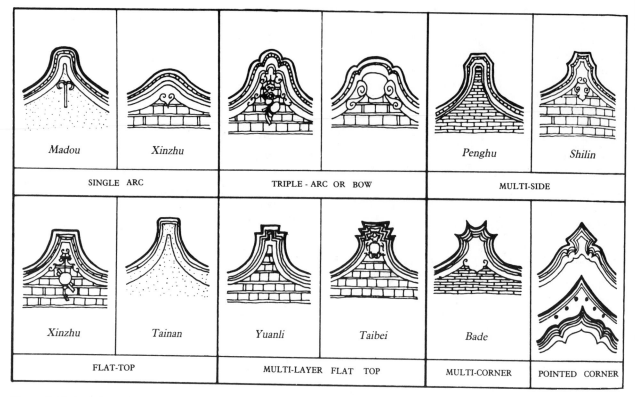

Figure 4.16. A variety of gable profiles found on Taiwan.

sents a selection of the stylized gable profiles that appear on dwellings with a *mabei* (horseback) roof. For the most part, these profiles represent those found on substantial dwellings of the twentieth century, depicting arcuate, flat, and multiple-shaped forms. The variations in profile are further enhanced by decorative additions that usually express symbolic meanings related to the five elements (wood, fire, metal, water, and the earth) and the *yin-yang* concept. Similar symbolic representations are added to the gable area of *yanwei* (swallowtail) style dwellings. The linear ridge line of the horseback style, however, is not decorated to the same degree as the swallowtail style. Just as on most temples, some swallowtail-style dwellings have representations of spirited animals, auspi-

cious fruits, and other symbolic items placed along the ridge line or along the sweep of the swallow's tail. These figures are usually of molded mortar embellished with porcelain fragments.

Windows and Other Features

Windows usually are small and few in number on rural houses, as can be seen in many of the figures in this chapter, because their presence weakens the load-bearing capacity of the walls. Significantly, the small window size offers some protection from intruders and subtropical thundershowers as well as serving as the principal means of ventilating the interior. Furthermore, open doorways, broad eaves, and southerly orientation facilitate summer ventilation. On the negative side, the paucity of windows makes the inside rather dark. The use of vertical brick or stone bars further restricts the passage of light but does offer additional protection. In the past, plaited straw screens usually served as shades on the windows of common houses. Decorative panels as an architectural motif have been placed over the window openings of only the houses of the wealthy such as those found on the Lin manse in Banqiao or that originally in the Daan area of eastern Taibei belonging to the Antai Lins. In addition to the use of latticework patterns of either parallel thin strips of wood or crisscrossed mosaics, wooden panels carved three-dimensionally are found on better residences.

SUMMARY

Tributary to similar cultural patterns found in southeastern China, the dwellings of Taiwan evolved under changing sociocultural circumstances. Not accepting Taiwan as domicile, early migrants built only shelter to meet their needs as sojourners. The construction of full-form dwellings subsequently accompanied the reclamation of land, the accumulation of wealth, and the decision to settle on the island. On Taiwan it is possible to examine the dwelling as humanized space that mirrors the family's size and structure and further proclaims the family's aspirations. Taking different forms, the house on Taiwan expresses functional and symbolic aspects. Its walls and layout define a variety of family sizes and patterns and acknowledge links to Chinese folk tradition. No striking structural elements separate dwellings on Taiwan from their precursors on the mainland, revealing clearly the adaptive quality of Chinese building practices that reach back to neolithic times. Even today throughout rural Taiwan, new dwellings are being built that evoke their patrimony by preserving the basic elements of the inherited folk culture.

CHAPTER 5

The Folk Tradition and the Built Environment

CHINESE buildings communicate components of a dynamic tradition which reveal Chinese cosmology and folk beliefs in practical terms. This has been true especially in the choice of sites, layout, construction process, and building of palaces, imperial graves, and even the walls of cities which themselves were considered "buildings." Similarly, although often in a less direct fashion, the nonpedigreed dwellings of China's masses imitate the cosmological predilections of the great tradition. The folk tradition, found in a great variety of forms throughout the country, infused housebuilding with practices that confirm the concerns of Chinese peasants for prosperity and happiness as well as protection against misfortune. Carpenters and masons, moreover, not only were able to incorporate charms to further invoke good fortune or dispel evil for the occupants of a house. They were also capable of inserting hexes.

Although Chinese records are rich in detailing the prescribed rites associated with the building of monumental architecture, documentation of the folk tradition in the raising of common houses on the China mainland is extremely limited for the past and virtually absent for the contemporary period. In Taiwan and Hong Kong, on the other hand, the resilience of the folk tradition in this realm is clearly observable even today in spite of rapid modernization. Since it is not possible here to elaborate upon this folk tradition in full, especially spatial and temporal variations, this chapter explores elements of the tradition which have affected the building of houses and which suggest the sociocultural milieu in which rural dwellings took form.

Fengshui: THE USES OF MYSTICAL ECOLOGY

Joseph Needham has expressed the spirit of Chinese architecture as one embodying "a feeling for cosmic pattern and the symbolism of the directions, the seasons, winds and constellations" (1971, 61). Chinese for more than a millennium have drawn upon the popular yet esoteric set of practices called *fengshui* in an attempt to integrate people, their activities, and nature. Literally "wind and water," *fengshui* encompasses an array of patterns and symbols to assist in the selection of proper sites for dwellings, palaces, cities, graves, roads, reservoirs, or even railway and power transmission lines. Basic to *fengshui* is the notion that human alterations of the landscape do not simply occupy empty space. Rather, building sites are viewed as manifesting certain properties which influence, even control, the fortunes of those who intrude upon the site. As explained by Maurice Freedman (1969, 7):

When a man puts up a building he inserts something into the landscape and between him and his neighbors. It follows that risks attend his enterprise and he must take precautions. The physical universe is alive with forces that, on the one side, can be shaped and brought to bear on a dwelling and those who live in it, and, on the other side, can by oversight or mismanagement be made to react disastrously. But the very act of siting and constructing a house to one's own advantage may be to the detriment of others. Modifications in the landscape reverberate. So that, in principle, every act of construction disturbs a complex system made up of nature and society, and it must be made to produce a new balance of forces lest evil follow.

Fengshui has enjoyed an enduring credibility within the Chinese cultural context. Its essence is a universe animated by the interaction of *yin* and *yang* in which an ethereal property known as *qi* ("life breath" or "cosmic energy") gives character and meaning to a place. Places may be spoken of at an elementary level as exemplifying either *yin* or *yang* characteristics, although sites often exhibit both traits simultaneously. *Yin* places express the female aspect, representing passivity and darkness, and frequently fall away from the sun to the north or northwest. They are optimal for burial (Knapp 1977 and 1982b). The male or *yang* characteristic expresses brightness and activity by serving the living as suitable sites for individual dwellings or even cities, facing generally south or southeast. To confuse these natural qualities is to invite adversity.

Accessibility to this mystical ecology is through the medium of a *fengshui shi* or *fengshui xiansheng*

("wind and water interpreter"), sometimes called a geomancer, who can perform the arcane monitoring of building sites. The typical *fengshui xiansheng* arms himself with a geomancer's compass *(luoban)* and manuals, as shown in Figure 5.1, for determining a proper building site. The *luoban* is a saucerlike block of wood which has at its center a south-pointing compass surrounded by more than

Figure 5.1. The selection of a building site by a geomancer and his assistants in a late Qing dynasty illustration.

a dozen concentric rings, each of which symbolically represents the ordering of Chinese metaphysics. These circular bands include, *inter alia,* the Eight Trigrams or *bagua,* the duodenary and sexagenary cycles, the location of the nine stars, the twenty-eight constellations, and the five agents (de Groot 1897, 959–975; Feuchtwang 1974, 18–95). Manipulating these complex rings, the geomancer is able to apply cosmology to matters as practical as house and grave siting. Essentially, as Freedman notes, "it is the geomancer's task to divine the potentialities of a given landscape and to bring them into relation with the future of the people who build in it" (1969, 12).

The *fengshui* characteristics of a site are linked to those who will utilize it by relating the time and date of the principal's birth to the particulars of the site. The temporal and spatial personalization of a site isolates for an individual and his family the fund of good fortune that accrues therefrom. In a world of limited resources, *fengshui* provides a means of assuring a reasonable share of good fortune that includes wealth, progeny, good harvests, and official positions.

Classical notions of siting, external orientation, and internal morphology that apply to Chinese buildings and relate to *fengshui* can be seen best in imperial capitals (Wright 1977, 47ff). As an expression of cosmic geometry, imperial capitals were laid out in the form of a four-sided figure, generally square, set beneath a round heaven. Each walled city symbolized aspects of imperial ideology, affirming the centrality of China in the world and the relationship between heaven and earth. Symbolism placed the emperor at the pivot of the cosmos within the microcosm of the universe itself: the walled imperial city. Cities were oriented to the cardinal directions and set so that they faced south, the direction associated with *yang,* the sun and life-giving forces. Directions

were correlated with symbols that animate *fengshui* and permeate all levels of Chinese culture. To the east was the azure dragon and the element wood emblemizing spring and the rising sun. To the south was the vermilion phoenix and the element of fire indicating summer. To the west was the white tiger and the element of metal symbolizing autumn and harvest. Completing the cycle in the north was the black tortoise and the element water indicating winter. Man was anchored in the soil or earth, the fifth element, found in the center of the cosmic map.

As with imperial capitals, the building sites for dwellings and graves, termed *xue* (literally "dragon's lair") and indicating an opening, were comprehended not only in relation to directions as defined by the sun; later aided by the compass, they were determined after probing the topographic surroundings. Using visible landscape features, the geomancer was able to define an auspicious site as one which modulated the flow of *qi,* the ethereal life breath of cosmic energy. Such a site ideally balanced "wind" and "water" and was one in which the *xue* was embraced by *sha,* distinguishable patterns in the contours of the earth such as ridges and also the banks of watercourses. Even the presence of boulders was noted. The undulations of intersecting ranges sheltered the site and symbolized the commingling of the azure dragon on the east (*yang*) and the white tiger on the west (*yin*).

Building sites were selected after considering the shapes of local landscape features representing the five elements of wood, fire, metal, water, and earth. A *fengshui* manual dictates that:

On a rock hill you must take an earthy site; on an earth hill you must take a rocky site. Where it is confined, take an open place; where it is open, take a confined space. On a prominence, take the flat; where it is flat, take the prominent. Where strong comes, take weak; where weak comes, take strong. Where there are many hills, emphasize water; where there is much water, emphasize hills. [Shanghai xingxiang 1957, 63; quoted in March 1968, 258]

As characterized further in another manual: "Mountain and water are male and female. . . . If the dragon curls left, the water has to curl right; if the dragon curls right, the water has to curl left; the two embrace each other, and only then does the site coalesce" (Ye 1696, *ce* 1.12b; quoted in March 1968, 258).

Fengshui manuals include abundant diagrams portraying a multiplicity of terrain patterns that might be encountered. Figure 5.2 shows basic hill and water shapes related to the five elements, the recognition of which is a primary step in choosing an auspicious site. The patterned assemblages of these configurations are defined much as they are for graves, although for the residences of the living much more open sites are desired. Care is

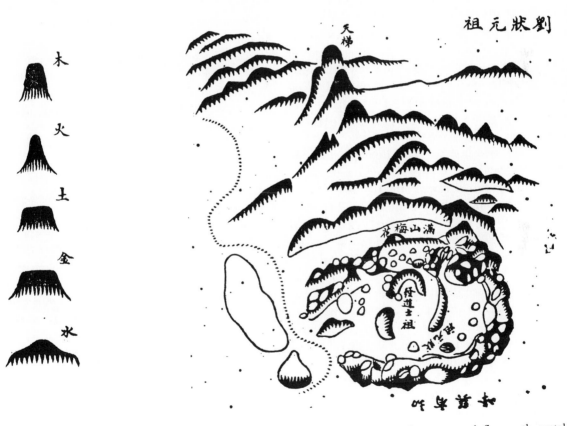

Figure 5.2. *Left:* Representations of hill shapes related to the five elements (from top to bottom, wood, fire, earth, metal, and water). *Right:* In this geomantic diagram, which combines a view from the ground with one from the air, the land of a successful degree candidate is presented. Prominent mountains flank the back; those on the side are lower and rim the site. A range of hills continues its reach from east to south but is at a tolerable distance. The dotted line indicates a stream. Specific sites for individual residences and graves must be located within this general geomantic landscape.

usually taken so that no part of the dwelling is shaded by hills on the east, south, or west, thus providing early sunrise and late sunset. This arrangement heightens the appearance of *yang,* the life-giving presence of the sun. Hills at the rear are thought necessary not only because they do not block the sun but because they also guard the rear flank. As succinctly stated in the *Yang zhai shishu* (Wang 1882): "To have the front high and the rear low is to be cut off with no family. With the rear high and the front low is to have oxen and horses." Commanding heights have always been avoided for the location of a house. With the building site *(xue)* selected, concern turns to the immediate environs of the prospective house for features that might influence the lives of those dwelling within. Figure 5.3 shows several situations, including the presence of a watercourse, pools, rocks, and trees, which presage good or bad fortune.

Much of canonical *fengshui* is comprehensible only to a cosmologically sophisticated geomancer who with "grand airs and literary pretensions . . . puts his metaphysic to common use" (Freedman 1969, 9). It is clear that those able to avail themselves of the geomancer's diagnostic expertise must possess at least a modicum of wealth in order to afford its application. Thus, the applications of *fengshui* described in the western-language literature on China invariably relate to the residences of gentry, merchants, and others of means. Although its full employment by the common peasant cannot be well documented, it is clear that because they too were concerned with worldly benefits and the avoidance of misfortune, they were frequently willing to give even of their meager resources to tap its benefits:

Underlying *fengshui* is a fundamental notion in and about Chinese society: all men . . . are in principle equal and may legitimately strive to improve their station in life. The peasant in his cottage has as much right to hope for advancement as the mandarin in his *yamen*. All men are morally entitled to take steps to raise themselves and their decendants—by scholarship, by the accumulation of riches, and by the religious pursuit of good fortune" [Freedman 1964, 125]

Observations of common houses in China confirm a widespread understanding by peasants of the attributes of *fengshui*. As Steven Bennett has noted (1978, 21): "Locating a good site is more than an exercise in cosmological abstraction and the manipulation of theoretical constructs; it is the successful application of cosmology to everyday life." The great range of topographic conditions throughout the country naturally militates against a single pattern of siting because the hilly areas of the south and the open plains of central and northern China present quite different environmental circumstances for the operation of *fengshui*. Yet it is clear that even uninitiated peasants sited dwellings in broad conformity with *fengshui* esoterica.

Practical considerations clearly underlay the ritualized behavior of *fengshui*. A south-facing slope that is protected on the northern side by a set of interlocking mountain ranges provides a building site open to the sun throughout the year and protected in winter from the cold winds characteristic of eastern Asia's climate. Earlier chapters indicate the extreme degree to which *zuobei chaonan*, "sitting north and facing south," came to be obligatory for Chinese dwellings, especially in the northern and central areas of the country. The orientation of the house may be seen as a device for obtaining the best advantage of sun and wind. Because the sun is regular in its path across the sky, the axial arrangement of a house controls the degree to which the heat of the sun is seasonally

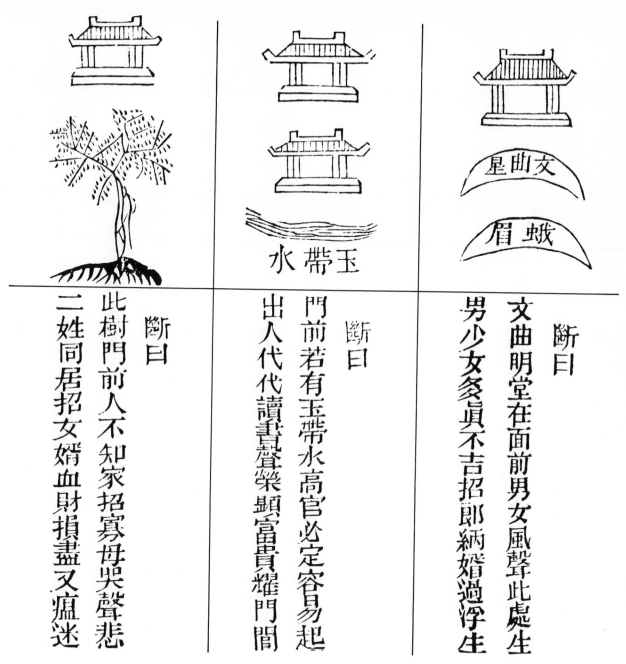

星助文　　　文曲明堂在面前男女風聲此處生

眉蛾　　　　男少女多貞不吉招郎納婿過浮生

断曰

門前若有玉帶水高官必定容易起

玉帶水　　　出人代代讀書聲榮顯富貴耀門間

断曰

此樹門前人不知家招寡母哭聲悲

二姓同居招女婿血財損盡又瘟迷

断曰

Figure 5.3. As these prescriptions indicate, the area in front of the entrance gate demands special attention. *Left:* With this tree, escaping people's notice, in front of the gate, this family is to have the vicissitude of sad wailing from a widowed mother. Two surnames shall dwell together here through taking in son-in-law. There is to be a total wasting away of hard earned wealth, pestilence, and bedevilment. *Center:* If there is a jade belt stream in front of the gate, this will give easy rise to high office. Begetting generation after generation of scholars will bring wealth and honor to glorify the house. *Right:* With certain ponds at the front, rumors of men and women will go forth from this place. Men will be few and women many, indeed a misfortune. This means livelihood will be earned by taking in husbands and sons-in-law.

captured or evaded. These natural conditions can be fine-tuned by the addition of overhanging eaves which block the high sun's rays in summer yet permit those of the low sun of winter to enter.

Working with nature, the practical peasant avoided marshy areas and built where drainage carried water away from the dwelling. Water, like mountain ranges, were seen as vital elements of a site. Peasants sought well-drained sites across which water coursed to meet their needs for irrigation, cooking, and washing, reflecting the advice of *fengshui* manuals for meandering streams, rather than fast-flowing ones, because they conducted good influences to a site. Peasants typically avoided cutting into a hill because of damage to the pulse of the dragon. *Fengshui* principles helped manage the use of an environment by underscoring elements of the natural order which had worked for generations of forebears.

Mountains are a metaphor for nature and therefore receive prominent attention in *fengshui* manuals. But since not all building sites are bounded by serpentine relief patterns, *fengshui* interpreters often were obliged to reach to the distant horizon in order to define the appropriate contours. In other cases, trees and bamboos were used as a substitute for the mountains in the background. In contrast to the west, where deciduous trees are planted in front of dwellings for summer shade, the norm in rural China has been to place trees behind where they function more as a windbreak. As mentioned in an earlier section, Chinese houses generally have windows only on the south-facing wall, leaving the rear and sides of the buildings closed to outside influences. It may be suggestive of modeling mountains that the narrow sides of houses throughout China that face east and west are called *shanqiang* ("mountain walls"), as shown in Figure 5.4.

With an appropriate orientation, the *gongting* or

main hall at the center of the building axis, overall symmetry, and a pair of flanking wings, the Chinese dwelling represents a concrete patterning of the natural features thought necessary to ensure good *fengshui*. Although less observable in small peasant homes, these features become more pronounced as the dwelling reaches full form.

ALMANACS, INSTRUMENTS, AND CHARMS: FOLK BELIEFS AND BUILDING

Experience nurtured recognition of the prospects, benign or perverse, that could emanate from

Figure 5.4. *Shanqiang,* the "mountain wall" gabled end of a rural dwelling, north of Beijing.

Plate 1. Set among the karst topography of the Guangxi Zhuang Autonomous Region in southern China, this compact village of adobe houses reveals a relatively consistent southerly orientation with each dwelling facing another's back side.

Plate 2. In the dry flatlands of the Ningxia Hui Autonomous Region, this large village is made up of generally south-facing tamped earth houses each with a commodious courtyard defined by a tamped earth wall.

Plate 3. In some villages, such as this one in eastern Zhejiang Province, the houses front on a canal.

Plate 4. With an extensive roof overhang which can be used for drying crops, some dwellings in Sichuan are isolated while many more are in compact hamlets.

Plate 5. Near Chengdu in western Sichuan, this thatched roof farmhouse is constructed of load-bearing walls of adobe brick.

Plate 6. Set among the verdant hills of Shangtianzhu near Hangzhou, Zhejiang province, these dwellings include tiled roofs and whitewashed tamped earth curtain walls set between the slender wood columns.

Plate 7. The load-bearing stepped gable walls, capped with tiled copings, are the most visually striking element of this dwelling in Wuxi, Jiangsu province.

Plate 8. This hillside earth-sheltered housing is faced with brick. The tamped earth wall is pierced by a substantial gate structure made of brick.

Plate 9. This modern brick house, situated in northern Shanxi province, utilizes abundant wood in the construction of its facade and rooms even though the surrounding area is very lightly wooded.

Plate 10. The *kang* or elevated bed which is connected via flues to the stove occupies the sunny southern side of many north China rural dwellings.

Plate 11. Loessial soil is shoveled into these shallow molds, compacted first with the feet and then with a stone rammer to form bricks at a site near Lanzhou, Gansu province. The bricks may be stacked immediately, as shown in the rear, for air drying in the autumn sun.

Plate 12. A moveable frame is used to form individual bricks from earth cut from the base of a paddy field, Guangxi Zhuang Autonomous Region.

Plate 13. Utilizing a *chuandou* frame, carpenters in the foothills of Emei mountain, Sichuan province, raise a new farmhouse.

geomantic decision making or its neglect. Once a building site was determined, a suitable date was needed to begin construction. Annual almanacs were produced throughout the mainland well into the twentieth century and in Hong Kong and Taiwan even today to help guide peasants through the calendrical labyrinth. During the imperial past, the production of the Chinese almanac was a state monopoly bearing the imprimatur of the Imperial Board of Astronomy. Almanacs not only contained important astronomical information for ritual purposes; they also aided the definition of the agricultural cycle and gave the common people knowledge about "the days and hours that are lucky for everything in life, from a wedding to taking a bath" (Couling 1917, 12). For building purposes such almanacs indicated the dates which should be chosen or avoided and even the lucky and unlucky times for the initial breaking of the earth *(dong tu),* raising a ridgepole *(shang liang),* installing a door *(an men),* and building a stove *(zuo zao).* Figure 5.5 depicts a contemporary almanac.

The observance of propitious dates for construction anticipates the injunction of a continuing battery of measures to prevent adversity and call forth good fortune. These measures include offerings and the use of charms and talismans. Formal rituals performed on the dictated dates accompanied the raising of the roof beam, often the most costly piece of building material in a country generally poor in timber. Sometimes painted red, an especially auspicious color, the beam would be lifted by the carpenters who attached charms and talismans to it as shown in Figure 5.6. Slips of red paper, usually in odd multiples bearing the character *fu* for happiness or expressive phrases that evoke the auspicious circumstances, can also be seen in the figure.

An early twentieth-century discussion reveals that, at least in one area of China, the carpenters "strike the beam several times with a hammer painted red. This hammer is afterwards presented by the master of the house to a man who has no son; and who if the wished-for-heir is later on born to him, is expected to reward the donor of the hammer by inviting him and his family to a feast" (von Poseck 1905, 352). In this way, the favorable circumstances of housebuilding redound even to those who assist. The sieve and mirror fixture which is hung from the beam is described as "charms, or anti-spectral devices, for the purpose of protecting from demons and warding off all evil influences" (Dore 1917–1918, 492) or, at least for the sieve alone, as a prophetic indication that "many children would be born in the house" (Baker 1979, 90). Grains of rice are sometimes strewn about or hung in small sacks from the ridgepole to evoke fertility and prosperity. Sometimes men's trousers and lanterns, which are homophonous with Chinese words for riches or sons, may be suspended as well.

The common dwellings of poorer peasants peasants usually were built with only their own labor and that of their kinsmen and neighbors. Even derivative renovation and expansion had a do-it-yourself aspect, but as structures increased in complexity, technical conditions often necessitated outsiders to do the work. Those with greater resources usually employed carpenters and masons who operated as both technicians and magicians. Their efforts at once heightened the prospects for good fortune while introducing the possibility of inflicting of damaging curses. Utilizing information transmitted to them through mnemonic rhymes in the oral tradition as well as from illustrated manuals, craftsmen paid great attention to sequences and measures. Purportedly deriving from Lu Ban, the patron of carpenters and bricklayers, these ideas established conven-

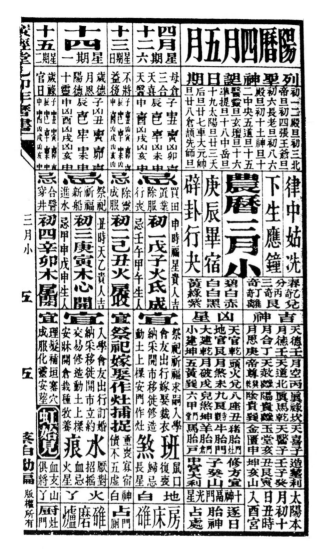

Figure 5.5. Hours and days to be chosen or avoided for building and other daily activities as represented in a contemporary almanac.

tions that were recorded in the fifteenth century *Lu Ban jing* (Lu Ban Manual) and have governed building practices and dimensions down to the present in Taiwan and Hong Kong. Carpenters used a special rule (*Lu Ban chi* or *wengongchi*) divided into eight segments each with four divisions. Utilized in determining the size of rooms as

well as the dimensions of windows and doors, the Lu Ban rule had the effect of standardizing measurements by virtue of avoiding those proportions which presaged misfortune (Guo 1981, 102–104). In Taiwan, the *wengongchi* also has been used to determine the depth of courtyards in proportion to the height of the ridgepole, the length of rafters, the size of tiles and bricks, and the dimensions of stoves, among other things (Seaman 1985).

Chinese folklore includes tales of carpenters and bricklayers using spells to curse a dwelling and its inhabitants because of low pay or disrespect. Carpenters used drawings or wooden figures, nailed to the ceiling or hidden above a beam, to effect a curse. The location of the nail indicated an affliction which would befall the family: "If it pierced the eyes, he would go blind; if it pierced the ears, he would become deaf; if it were through the mouth, he would become dumb; and if it penetrated the heart, then he would die from heart failure. If the figure were hammered onto the door, the master would often be absent and domestic harmony would be destroyed" (Kuo 1973, 46).

Bricklayers used similar hexes, although theirs

were usually made of clay. A well-known tale called "The Magic of the Mason" tells of disgruntled workmen who, because they were dissatisfied with the food provided them, made a small boat and boatman of clay which they secreted in the eaves of a new dwelling. The boat was made to face outward so that luck would be borne away from the house, leaving the occupants in poverty, until finally they no longer would have enough to eat. Quarrels and death, according to the tale, plagued the household and it was reduced to destitution. Many years later the master mason passed the house and was touched by the sincerity of the widow. He climbed a ladder and turned the prow of the boat around to initiate new prosperity for those living in the dwelling (Eberhardt 1965, 73–75).

Others believed that "a pair of clay figures sus-

Figure 5.6. Charms and talismans employed in the construction of a dwelling.

pended in the chimney by hairs from a horse's tail would cause quarrels between husband and wife as the hot air rising from the fire would cause the figures to swing and clash against each other. A clay knife pointed at the bedroom or the ancestral hall would lead to murders in the family" (Kuo 1973, 46). Figure 5.7, taken from the *Lu Ban jing jiang jia jing,* illustrates a variety of devices used by craftsmen to bring misfortune to a house and its inhabitants. Wariness of the tricks of masons and carpenters fostered the need for prescriptive prudence. As a result, all-purpose charms were used by those occupying a house to combat whatever curses the builders might have cast.

Once the dwelling was completed, it traditionally was believed necessary to continue the display of paper charms to ensure good fortune and ward off evil. Often this was done at the beginning of the annual cycle at the New Year when red papers would be affixed on the front door and nearby. Rather than countering misfortune, these charms elicited positive conditions. Either individually or in groups, the strips of red paper known as *wufu linmen* ("five blessings knocking at the door") might be pasted on the lintel. As single characters, these charms represent *fu* (happiness), *lu* (honors), *shou* (longevity), *xi* (joy), and *cai* (wealth).

Traditionally couplets also were affixed at the New Year on either side of the door. As depicted in Figure 5.8, they continue to be used through-out China today as expressions of hope. Added sometimes as antidotes for evil influences that might arise from location or subsequent nearby building are mirrors and the Eight Trigrams or *bagua* symbol. The mirror, radiating *yang,* is usually hung above the door where it has been regarded by many Chinese as a potent deflector of malevolent influences. Protection may be enhanced by affixing to the doors a pair of *menshen* or door gods as shown in Figure 5.9. Facing each other and in full battle garb, these fierce warriors are to ensure the safety and inviolability of the dwelling. Especially common with urban houses but found with village dwellings as well are *yingbi,* also called *zhaobi,* or spirit walls of brick or wood. Placed just inside the gate, the *yingbi* is believed by some Chinese to be capable of deflecting negative elements.

These exterior charms and measures usually were accompanied by additional gods and talismans inside the house as further precaution, such as the Zaojun, the Kitchen God shown in Figure 5.10. Presiding over the domestic hearth, Zaojun served as a guarantor of household harmony and symbol of household unity. Just prior to the New Year, the paper image of Zaojun would be burned, sending the god to the Emperor of Heaven to report on the family members' behavior over the past year. He returned to the house on New Year's eve with the pasting up of a new picture of him to begin anew another annual tour of

---

Figure 5.7. This page from a manual for carpenters illustrates charms that could be used to bring misfortune or fortune to the residents. Of the twelve charms listed, only four are auspicious (numbers 3, 7, 9, and 11). Number 7 tells that placing two copper coins face down on each end of the main beam will ensure wealth in the family. The same condition can be accomplished by placing rice grains on the roof brackets according to number 11. Number 9 indicates that concealing a brush and ink stick in the beams will guarantee high office. The remaining eight charms indicate curses. Number 1 reveals that burying an ox bone under the house will bring about lives of hard work and misery; not even a coffin will be available when the head of the household dies. Number 2, showing hair tied around a knife, when hidden under the threshold ensures the loss of the husband and that sons will become monks. According to number 10, placing a white tiger on the beam above the door, facing inward, will assure much family quarrel, sickness for the womenfolk, and death for the wife.

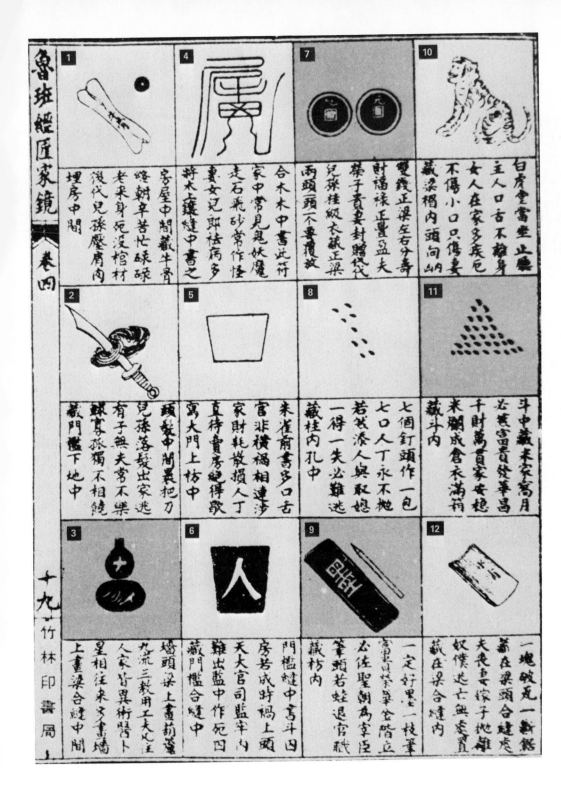

魯班鏡匯家鏡　卷四

十九　竹林印書局

1
房屋中間藏牛骨
絡朝辛苦忙碌碌
老來身破沒棺材
後代兒孫歷膚肉
埋房中間

4
合木木中畫此符
家中常見鬼妖魔
走石飛砂常作怪
妻女兒即祛病多
將木上鑲嵌中畫之

7
雙鐵正梁左右分壽
財福祿禒丞豐盈夫
蔡子貴妻封贈代代
兒孫掛級衣藏正梁
兩頭頭不要露敌

10
白房堂富豐止廳
主人口舌不離身
女人在家多疾厄
不傷小口只傷妻
埋梁楣內頭向峒

2
頭髮中間裏把刀
錄寡孫獨不相饒
有子無夫常不樂
兒孫落髮出家逃
藏門檻下地中

5
寫大門上枋中
直待賣房絕得歇
家財耗散損人丁
官非積禍相連涉

8
七個釘頭作一包
七口人丁永不抛
若筴添人與取惚
一得一失必難逃
藏桂內孔中

11
斗中藏米家寫月
必藏富田貴發華昌
千財萬貫家安穩
米關成倉衣滿箱
藏斗內

3
九流三教用工夫
人家皆異術醫卜
皇相往來多畫墙
上畫梁合縫中間

6
門檻縫中畫斗四
天大官司監牢內
房若成時禍上頭
牆頭梁上畫葫蘆
藏門檻合縫中

9
一定好黑七一枝筆
富貴日榮華金階立
必佐聖朝為室臣
筆頭若蛙退官職
藏枋內

12
一塊破瓦一斷鋸
菖在梁頭合建處
夫妻喜冤子地離
奴僕逃亡無處覓
藏在梁合縫內

Figure 5.8. Couplets pasted on the door at New Year's time frame the gateway of a peasant house in southern Hebei province.

surveillance and protection. A stone pillar inscribed with the characters *shi gandang* ("stone dares to resist evil") or *Taishan shi gandang* ("stone of Mount Tai dares to resist evil") might be placed near the house to serve as an external line of defense. Taken collectively, these charms portray a desire to make the inner space of family life inviolate by keeping at bay those malevolent ele-

Figure 5.9. Full-color depictions of door gods pasted on the two leaves of an entry door near Guangzhou, Guangdong province.

ments belonging to a different spatial domain (Guan 1980, 180).

Figure 5.10. Represented either by characters indicating the name Zaojun or by an image similar to this picture from the mid-1950s, the Kitchen God was affixed above the cooking stove. Symbolic of family unity, Zaojun maintained domestic harmony and reported each year to his superiors on the activities of family members.

SUMMARY

The common Chinese house traditionally has been more than a vessel for daily life and a haven from the changing forces of nature. Throughout much of Chinese history, sites were selected and dwellings built based upon images of an organic view of the cosmos that included even the mundane tasks associated with providing a habitat. To what extent such traditional belief systems and practices still directly affect building decisions on the China mainland is not clear. There are indications, however, that as in Taiwan, Hong Kong, and Singapore such predilections continue to guide construction. Such structured efforts manifest the Chinese folk tradition as well as demonstrate those factors which tie the individual, family, and society and link them symbolically to the past. Utilizing the practice of *fengshui,* builders have sought to insure prosperity and protect against misfortune. Recognizing and employing auspicious and inauspicious numbers and directions, builders and "wind and water interpreters" presumably have been able to warrant to those living in a household the long-term benefits that accrue to a specific site and dwelling layout. Not incidentally, the rudiments of *fengshui* reveal as well a clear understanding of local environmental conditions, especially as these relate to sun angle, drainage, and prevailing winds.

CHAPTER 6

Rural Housing in Contemporary China

THE Chinese government acknowledged a critical housing problem in the countryside by the end of the 1970s. Although gross agricultural output value had nearly quadrupled between 1949 and 1980, rapid population growth had brought about only slight increases and in some cases actual decreases in per capita production of farm products with only a "sluggish improvement" in peasant living standards (Yu 1984, 213). With limited resources, most peasants were unable to bring about appreciable improvement in either the quality or quantity of their rural housing in the thirty years following the founding of the People's Republic. In many cases, as Fei Hsiao-tung (Fei Xiaotong) discovered in his restudy of Kaixiangong in 1981, "not only are most of the villagers living in the same houses in which they lived in 1936, but those houses now appear rather more dilapidated than in 1936 and are providing shelter for a much larger number of people" (Fei 1983, 204).

Aware of the need to formulate new housing policies, the Ministry of Urban and Rural Construction and Environmental Protection announced in 1984 a comprehensive nationwide survey of rural and urban housing. Initiated on July 1 and completed by December 31, 1985, the survey inventoried inherited housing stock, listed recent construction, and noted problems of design and scarce building materials. No date was set for publication of the findings nor was the purpose of the survey clarified beyond stating that it will provide data for formulating social development programs and aid in the solution of housing problems throughout the country ("Housing Survey" 1985; Li 1984, 1). Awaiting the statistical and descriptive results of this survey, it is possible in the interim to gain insight into the current status of rural housing through a combination of field observation, statements in the press expressing official policy, and general reports of construction activity in the countryside.

Field observations corroborate Chinese press accounts since 1980 of a rural housing boom as well as concern at all levels for improvement in general living standards throughout the country. It is recognized officially, however, that although "living standards have improved, levels are low and not even" (Li and Zhang 1982, 15). The Chinese mark the convening in December 1978 of the

Third Plenary Session of the Eleventh Central Committee of the Chinese Communist Party as the critical juncture in redressing errors in economic policy which had frustrated the improvement of living standards. Earlier policies, the Chinese now admit, not only erroneously limited state investment in nonproductive capital construction projects, such as housing, but also fettered economic initiatives which might have made it possible for peasants themselves to improve their quality of life. It is claimed that especially during the Cultural Revolution between 1966 and 1976 projects that directly affected people's lives, such as housing, education, and health, were "starved of funds" with state investment at only one-third of acceptable levels (Yu 1984, 11).

In addressing problems which had been "left unresolved for years," not only were state investment patterns altered but a number of major measures were set forth to stimulate the rural economy and raise peasant income. The implementation of new agricultural policies beginning in late 1979 may be summarized as follows (Zhan and Liu 1984, 209ff):

1. Production teams, usually composed of related individuals or neighbors, have been granted the right to decide what to cultivate and to determine measures for increasing production in a contract or responsibility system.
2. Farm income has been tied directly to production according to principles of "to each according to his work."
3. State purchase prices for farm products have been raised.
4. Private plots have been increased to as much as fifteen percent of total cultivable area.
5. Domestic sideline activities, including commodity production, have been encouraged to supplement income from collective sources.
6. In addition to grain production, diversified cash crops suitable to local conditions have been encouraged.
7. Village fairs and farm produce markets have been promoted as outlets for peasant production.

The implementation of these measures quickly brought about a dramatic growth of agricultural, sideline, and rural industrial production, resulting in a pronounced expansion of peasant income. Sample surveys conducted by the State Statistical Bureau since 1978 suggest not only the direction but also the magnitude of the changes. Table 6.1 indicates that during this period there was a small decrease in the number of residents per sampled household at the same time there was a forty percent increase in the number of rooms per household. These changes led to a startling fifty percent increase in the room area for each resident between 1978 and 1984. At the same time, the percentage of expenditures for food, clothing, fuel, and recreation decreased while the outlay for housing more than tripled (Guojia tongji ju 1985, 102–103).

The *Beijing Review* summed up developments by stating: "It's a tradition among Chinese peasants to build houses when they have money to spare." In 1980, the journal continued, "about 5 million peasant families throughout the country built new houses or rebuilt old ones" ("Rural Housing Boom" 1981). By 1982 nearly one in three households was involved in expansion of their living space. In many other cases, renovation was taking place in anticipation of later enlargement of the dwelling. Total floor space of *new* housing construction from 1979 to 1985, according to the results of a sample survey conducted by the State Statistical Bureau, averaged 5.5 square meters per person in rural areas (Li

Table 6.1. Rural Housing Changes: 1978–1984

	1978	1979	1980	1981	1982	1983	1984
Number of households surveyed	6,095	10,282	15,914	18,529	22,775	30,427	31,375
Number of residents/household	5.73	5.65	5.53	5.5	5.45	5.43	5.37
Average number of new rooms built/household	0.11	0.22	0.23	0.27	0.29	0.31	0.25
Average number of rooms/household	3.64	3.84	4.06	4.28	4.56	4.81	5.07
Average room area per person (square meters)	10.17	11.03	11.59	12.47	13.41	14.25	15.38

Source: "Sample Survey" (1983, 22); Guojia tongji ju (1985, 102).

1985, 18). The Chinese press regularly reports that more rural housing has been built in the past six years than in the previous thirty years. Average per capita rural floor space has been raised to 13.6 square meters, almost triple that for urban residents. This figure, however, masks considerable variation in China's countryside (Xu Zhengzhong 1985, 1).

Heralded in the Chinese press and clearly observable on the ground, the long-overdue renewal of rural housing stock for so many of the approximately 175 million rural households in such a short period of time is a significant episode in China's architectural history. Newly built rural dwellings reveal patterns of continuity mixed with change. The strength of precedent continues to play a compelling role in the design and construction of rural housing. Nonetheless, transformations in several aspects of Chinese life since 1949 have brought about pronounced deviations from traditional norms. This chapter highlights some of the factors which have guided the emergence of current rural housing patterns.

HOME OWNERSHIP

Although land in China is owned either by the collectives (such as production brigades or communes) or directly by the state, the constitution guarantees the right of citizens to own their own houses ("Constitution" 1983, 14). Private home ownership is widespread in China's countryside where peasants build, bequeath, sell, expand, renovate, or partition dwellings as they choose. In some cases, the collective may build houses and rent them to its members. This practice is in striking contrast to the housing situation in urban areas where only a small percentage of housing is privately owned; most is municipally owned or owned by units such as factories or educational institutions (Kirkby 1985, 166–167; Ma 1981, 228–229). State-owned urban housing is apportioned to work units which allocate it to their employees. Urban rents typically do not exceed five percent of income and are determined according to a scale which takes into account the type of building, amount of space occupied, and location (Fang and Chen 1980).

Since 1984, the Chinese press has reported on the need to reform urban housing patterns to mitigate shortages and end inequities. In 1984, the average living space for each urban resident was calculated at 4.8 square meters—two-thirds less than in sampled rural households yet a one-third increase from the 3.6 square meters in 1978 ("Solving" 1985). These averages conceal considerable variation and often represent only a regaining of the average living space figures of the early 1950s (Xu Yuanchao 1985, 1). By the year 2000, current plans are to expand urban housing to allow for 8 to 12 square meters per person as well as a flat for each family ("Shortages" 1985).

Excessively low urban rents, it is now believed, have strained state resources and provided insufficient capital to improve maintenance and management or to undertake additional construction. Pilot programs have been instituted in many cities to generate capital for new housing construction by selling flats and freestanding houses to individuals. According to official reports, some 1.9 million square meters of housing was sold to private buyers in 1984 in 111 cities and 200 counties across the country, an increase of ninety-one percent over 1983 ("Flat Sales" 1985, 7). Even with these tentative steps toward commercialization, urban housing nonetheless remains largely in the hands of the state, municipalities, and work units.

The widespread private ownership of rural dwellings is not only a consequence of the redistribution of the property of landlords after 1949; it also reflects historical conditions that have left peasants free to build shelter according to their means. A survey in north China in the late 1920s showed that even if peasants had to rent all the land necessary to produce their sustenance, they usually owned their dwellings (Gamble 1954, 49). For the most part simple cottages were without deeds and "ownership" was acknowledged by occupancy; more substantial dwellings, however, did have deeds. The additive character of basic vernacular Chinese dwellings permitted extensions to accommodate normal cycles of family expansion. With contractions in the domestic unit, portions of the dwelling could be transferred to others for their use. Inheritance and division of the household head's property were guided by customary law (Shuzo 1978, 109–150).

Ownership of rural dwellings today is substantiated through the record keeping of the collective; adjustments in title are made if a transfer by sale, gift, or death occurs. By regulation, the construction of new housing on land not previously occupied by an individual's dwelling must be approved by the collective. It is clear that such approval often has been given with little concern for overall planning; indeed, many compact residential areas have been allowed to grow in a somewhat chaotic manner. Furthermore, the press from time to time mentions the illegal expansion of rural housing onto family plots and contracted farmland even without the acquiescence of the collective.

Settlement Patterns, Rural Planning, and Housing Design

Natural villages in China largely emerged over a long period of time as the rural population increased under conditions of small-scale agriculture. Viewed from the perspective of the composition of dwellings, traditional Chinese villages may be described as nucleated or dispersed. The layout of dwellings in both dispersed and nucleated villages arose from largely unplanned circumstances and reflected individual concerns rather than rational land use. This was especially true where dwellings originally were sited according to *fengshui* and where additions were made to accommodate changes in family needs.

The recent development strategies which have guided the restructuring of so much of China's countryside into geometrically regular patterns reflect a desire to bring about a rural-urban convergence. In attempting to reduce the difference between the urban and rural areas, policies have promoted what might be termed a partial "urbanization" of agricultural areas through the spatial concentration of housing and subsidiary industrial production and the provision of a range of services not normally expected in farm areas. The degree to which these changes affect the countryside varies from *xian* to *xian* and depends to a high degree on local decisions. Model communities have been popularized through the press and through the distribution of handbooks for rural redevelopment.

Although the social transformation of China's countryside by 1960 had restructured land tenure arrangements and markedly altered field patterns, little attempt was made at the time to change the layout of rural residential sites. In pursuit of rationalized land use, fragmented landholdings were consolidated and grave sites leveled to create a less chaotic geometry in the countryside, but the disarray of housing was little considered except in a number of vanguard communes. In the early 1970s a few advanced communes and production brigades in widely scattered locations began systematic spatial reorganization that sub-

Figure 6.1. Formalized plan of Quantangzi, Hunan province. Rows of residences are oriented south, each facing a road.

sequently altered the nature of the rural dwelling in the areas under their administration.

Figure 6.1 portrays the results of the reorganization and rebuilding of Quantangzi commune, Hunan province, which occurred between 1971 and 1974. With eleven production brigades, 2,732 households, and a population of 12,959 living in irregularly sited dwellings, the map of the commune was redrawn to include a gridded and compartmentalized plan that maintained a dispersed pattern of settlement. Without speaking of other land use, it can be seen clearly that residential hamlets for the production teams were transformed into 102 similar sets of longitudinal row houses, 101 of which were oriented due south (Jiang et al. 1984, 17–18). The number of individual dwellings or households in each row-house complex cannot be determined from the information available.

Similarly, as shown in Figure 6.2, the spatial realignment of a production brigade with four production teams in Hebei province resulted in a structured nucleated village whose symmetrical geometry is reminiscent of the plan of an ancient Chinese capital city. Axial symmetry, orientation to the cardinal directions, centrally located administration, parallel rows of housing facing due south—all are traditional urban planning concepts adapted to rural use. Furthermore, the settlement is ringed by a wall, but in this case the wall is a double row of trees rather than earth and stone. Instead of wards, each division comprises a production team.

Many other compact villages on the north China plain have been rebuilt in recent decades in order to reduce the amount of land occupied by housing and provide a more planned community. An example is Liuminying, a village located south of Beijing. In 1975 Liuminying began a transformation to a "new village" *(xincun)*. By

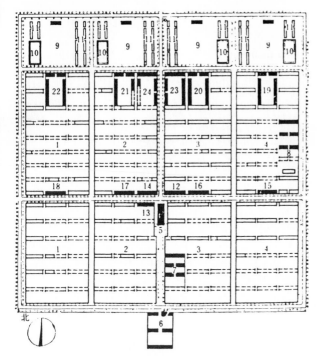

Figure 6.2. Contemporary plan of four production teams in Hebei province. Oriented north and south with intersecting roads and ringed by a wall of trees, this layout is reminiscent of a traditional capital city. The housing areas of each production team are numbered 1, 2, 3, and 4. At the center of each housing area is a brigade activity center (15, 16, 17, and 18). Each team has its own grain-drying area (9), water storage pond (10), and pigpens (11) as well as livestock pens (19, 20, 21, and 22). Shared facilities include a meeting hall (5), school (6), youth dormitory (7), reception center (8), headquarters (12), retail shop (13), health center (14), equipment service station (23), and sideline production center (24).

1980 the press was reporting that "the people of Liuminying had completely rebuilt their village from the former mess of dilapidated farmhouses scattered haphazardly between crooked rutty lanes" (Liu Chenlie 1980, 16). The planning principles that underlie these new villages mimic those of urban areas. These concepts include axial symmetry, intersecting road grids, parallel rows of housing all facing due south, and centrally located administrative offices and services. Often the appearance is less that of a village than it is of a residential section of a small town except for the presence of pigs and chickens as well as grain drying on the roadways. An aerial view of a new settlement in Gansu province illustrates these characteristics (Figure 6.3). By the middle of 1985, it was reported by the Ministry of Urban and Rural Construction and Environmental Protection that fully seventy-five percent of rural villages and towns had formulated plans for the orderly arrangement of buildings and conservation of land. It was optimistically predicted that by the end of the year such rural planning would be completed for the whole country (Xiao 1985, 1).

Efforts to consolidate dispersed dwellings into a nucleated and planned rural settlement go beyond the desire to conserve building space. Compact villages further facilitate the provision of services that not only include health stations, schools, post offices, theaters, and public bathhouses but also

Figure 6.3. Axial symmetry, intersecting road grids, and parallel rows of south-facing dwellings are found in a new settlement in a recently reclaimed area of Gansu province.

make it possible to provide running water, drainage, and electricity to individual households. Currently only five percent of Chinese rural residents enjoy piped water in their dwellings with this increasing to as much as thirty-four percent in a well-developed province such as Zhejiang (Xiao 1985, 1; Zhang 1985, 179; "Zhejiang" 1985, 3). Most households, as in other areas of the developing world, take water from deep wells, streams, or common stand pipes even in nucleated settlements. Handbooks for rural development in China give prominent attention to low-cost schemes for providing water to such new rural communities not only for convenience but also to reduce health problems (Jiang et al. 1984, 121–150; Gao and Zeng eds. 1982, 181–200). These include conventional water towers and small low-cost pressure tanks to distribute the water. The provision of these services to rural areas is seen as an important step in reducing the differences between the country and the city that will further facilitate the expansion of nonagricultural activities in the countryside.

Not all rural settlements, of course, have been redrawn and rebuilt. Where planning has been weak or dilatory, many peasants have been expanding the size of their houses or building new dwellings on nearby farmland as they have done in the past. The magnitude of this tendency to seize farmland to build houses and its relationship to family planning was brought home in a manual for rural planners: "If each of the several million production teams in the country were to newly occupy only one *mu* (0.066 hectare) of cultivable land for new housing, this would mean that several million *mu* of such land would be removed from production" (Gao and Zeng 1982, 19). Concern for such irrational use of land in a country where the per capita amount of arable land is currently only about 0.1 hectare, having decreased

by about eleven percent since 1957, led the State Council to pass a regulation calling for rural planning and specifying that only old residential sites, hilly areas, and unproductive land be used for dwellings (Zhao Ziyang 1983, 182). To strengthen rural land management, a state land law is being prepared that will provide legal sanctions against those violating constraints on building on arable land (Nie 1985, 3).

NEW RURAL HOUSING

The variety of newly constructed rural housing reflects not only the duplication of traditional dwelling styles but also the introduction of designs that strikingly break with tradition. In some cases, such as with active solar houses, truly revolutionary design changes have found their way into China's countryside. With 1.5 billion square meters of new housing built during 1978–1981 and 2.5 billion square meters estimated for 1981–1985, it is impossible to detail here the full variety of rural housing throughout the country (Zhao Bonian 1983, 52; "Construction" 1985). In 1984, a particularly busy year for construction, fifty percent of new housing was of kiln-dried brick and wood frame construction, twenty percent varied frameworks, with less than fifteen percent of earth and thatch (Xiao 1985, 1).

Freestanding, single-story houses (*pingfang*) located in dispersed villages not undergoing consolidation are most likely to be reconstructed using the traditional styles common to the areas in which they are found. For the most part, such houses retain traditional form but are improved in terms of materials and size. Common shapes characterize poor dwellings as well as those of rich farmers; moreover, such dwellings may be differentiated by the materials of their construction. As the economic circumstances of the household improves, the dwelling may be upgraded through the use of wooden walls, plastering, kiln-dried brick, and tile roofs.

New construction at the foot of Emei mountain in the Chengdu basin of western Sichuan province offers several examples. Plate 13 shows the construction of the wooden *chuandou* framework of a large farmhouse. Using the abundant timber from nearby hillsides, a carpenter team from the brigade, as shown in Figures 6.4 and 6.5, fashions the poles and interlocking beams for a frame not unlike those supporting large traditional palaces as well as common houses in many parts of the country. Built as an addition to a section only recently completed, the new construction nearly doubles the size of the dwelling as seen in Figure 3.48. Typical of houses in this area of copious rainfall, the slope of the roof is more pronounced and there is a more generous overhang than in most other parts of China. A major addition is the use of half-burnt gray tiles for the roof as an improvement over common thatching. Nearby, smaller improved houses of similar structure and roofing have like walls of wood and plaster, favored over adobe. (Compare Figures 2.40 and 2.41.) Many of these houses are modest with pounded earth floors and paper windows, parts which can be improved later as the resources of the peasant family allow.

In a compact but unstructured village on the outskirts of Guilin in Guangxi Zhuang Autonomous Region of southern China, reconstructed dwellings are being improved by substituting locally produced red clay bricks for adobe as can be seen by comparing Figures 3.7 and 3.8. On the fringe of the residential area, the brigade brickmaking team digs the lateritic soil, pounds it into forms, and stacks the bricks to sun dry for a week before firing them in large coal-fired kilns as shown in Figures 3.17 to 3.19. Brick making

Figure 6.4. The carpenter uses a hatchet to roughly dress the surface of a log to a smoothness that does not require planing.

Figure 6.5. A log set on two trestles is being measured to form one of the columns for this *chuandou* frame.

Figure 6.6. Han-style five-bay house and adjacent yurt north of Hohhot, Inner Mongolia.

occurs amid the rice fields and graveyards, leaving a pockmarked landscape for later leveling and terracing.

This volume has not discussed the variety of traditional dwellings occupied by any of the fifty-five national minority groups in China; instead I have emphasized the multiplicity of types occupied by the Han Chinese majority. Although many minority groups even today maintain dwellings in the traditional style, some have adopted Han house types. On the grasslands of Inner Mongolia north of the capital of Hohhot, some Mongols who have become sedentary have adopted the Han style five-bay house as shown in Figure 6.6. Built adjacent to a yurt which is now used for storage, the brick dwelling is oriented due south with windows only on the southern side, leaving solid walls as defense against the fierce winter and spring winds of the open plain. Such dwellings maintain the preferred Han siting principle of *zuobei chaonan* ("back to the north, face to the south"). The chimneys ventilate the *kang* beds used throughout these colder areas of northern China.

Figure 6.7 shows a similar farmhouse under construction in northern Shanxi province, about 10 kilometers from Datong. In an area where timber is not easily available, all the materials are from the earth except the wood used to frame the doors and windows. Adobe and kiln-dried brick are commonly used, as is the readily available local stone. The walls directly support the precious wooden roof beams, upon which a roof comprising a reed mat and a dirt and lime composition is laid. Figure 2.8 depicts a completed Han dwelling in an adjacent area, highlighting the decoration of the south-facing facade with colored paper that brightens the monochrome of the dusty surroundings.

With freestanding houses, a defined courtyard is not a prominent component although one is sometimes outlined by the use of a low stone or stalk fence to expand storage space for straw and faggots for burning. Each is individually sited and constructed according to traditional understandings of summer and winter sun angle and exposure as well as prevailing winds. In some cases road frontage is a consideration, but in many cases such houses are situated within the fields themselves and connected to a road only by narrow dirt paths. Found widely in regions where hills, canals, and streams dissect an area into separate parcels of land, isolated farmsteads are found as well in extensive dry regions as in northern Shanxi and Inner Mongolia. Individual dwellings can adapt themselves to the vagaries of topography to maximize effective land use. In a small number of cases, a cluster of freestanding or semidetached dwellings, or a series of like houses with common end walls, have been built in a "new village" *(xincun)* such as that of Huaxi brigade, Yin *xian,* Jiangsu province (Gao and Zeng 1982, 80–81).

Where there is a need to reduce the amount of land given over to housing, many new dwellings are being built *up* with two or three stories instead of expanding outward. Found throughout the country, these *loufang* (multistoried dwellings) are especially adaptable to the warmer and wetter southern portions of the country where ventila-

Figure 6.7. Load-bearing walls of kiln-dried brick and stone support the roof purlins directly on this small farmhouse under construction in northern Shanxi.

Figure 6.8. A multistoried dwelling of fired brick and tile near Linxian, Henan province.

tion is a major consideration, although they are being built widely in the north as well (Figure 3.61). Approximately fifty percent of new dwellings built in Wuxi, Jiangsu province, and in similar prosperous areas in recent years have been multistoried (Guowuyuan 1984, 49, 98–105). Many of these houses include a pigsty, courtyard, and kitchen as part of the first floor with the bedrooms above on the second floor, as seen in the substantial detached dwelling in rural Henan province in Figure 6.8. In southern China, as seen in Figure 6.9, south-facing balconies and open spaces which can be used for sideline production front the *loufang*. As in expanding *pingfang* (single-story houses), one section of the *loufang* is preferred for the use of the senior generation in a two-generation household. In this case, it is the airy and dry upper story. In 1985 alone, fifteen percent of all new housing in China's countryside was two or three stories. By 1990, the figure is expected to reach twenty percent (Zhu 1986, 1).

Where contemporary design considerations are given to village reconstruction, the favored form is a row-house development with courtyards. As mentioned earlier in this chapter, reorganized and geometrically precise villages have been built in many areas of the country especially since 1970. For the most part, the early construction of row houses was "designed" by local groups drawing on Chinese experience in small town developments. An example is found in Fenghuo, Liquan *xian,* Shaanxi province, the transformation of which took place in the middle to late 1970s (Figure 6.10). Set on the valley floor just below dwellings carved into the face of the loessial hillsides, the long east-to-west series of two-story row houses imitates a line of cave dwellings with their arcuate facades (Figure 6.11).

Unlike common dwellings in north China, the courtyard in this case has been placed in the rear rather than in the front. An innovation in this advanced brigade is the narrow alley which runs between the row houses, clearly shown in Figure 6.10. This alley provides access to the rear courtyards for delivery of the abundant material to be burned in the *kang* as well as removal of garbage and manure from the pigs raised by each household. This arrangement allows for a much more orderly front lane than is normally found in a Chinese village. The back courtyard includes not only the pigpen and a storage area for firewood and brush but also the latrine and bathing area. Figure 6.12 reveals the courtyard divided into two parts by walls of pounded earth capped with tiles to lessen weathering.

A shortcoming of a layout with dwellings placed back-to-back is that only half of them can have a southern exposure at the front of the house. On the other hand, the rest of the houses have a southern exposure for their back courtyards and have the sun in their back windows. While there may appear to be equity in this situation, the presence of windows on both front and

Figure 6.9. Row houses in the rural suburbs of Shanghai provide ventilation in front and back. Balconies overlook open spaces.

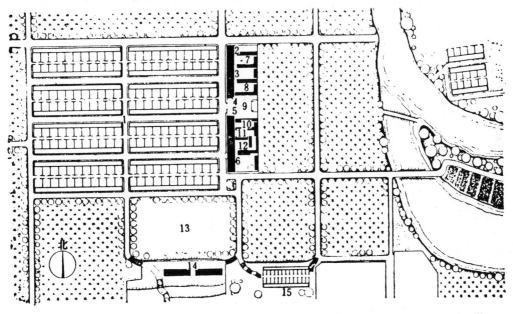

Figure 6.10. Plan of the Fenghuo brigade, Liquan *xian,* Shaanxi province. Eight pairs of two-story row dwellings comprise the residential area (1). Shown in heavy black rectangles are the agricultural technical station (2), cultural center (3), assembly hall (4), administrative headquarters and shop (5), hostel (6), equipment repair station (7), grain mill (8), open-air assembly area (9), health center (10), meeting room (11), dining hall (12), grain drying area (13), school (14), and pigstys (15).

Figure 6.11. The facades of new two-story brick row houses in Fenghuo brigade are patterned after the cave dwellings that were formerly used.

Figure 6.12. Rear courtyards of the row dwellings, Fenghuo brigade, Shaanxi province.

back walls exposes the houses to the direct blast of winter winds and spring dust storms. A striking break from this north/south pattern of exposure is to be found in the public buildings, all of which have their principal orientation toward the west. This location cannot be explained easily, given the easy availability of building land to the north and south of the housing.

A design that maintains traditional orientation is the block housing found in Qiliying, Henan province. Here, as shown in Figure 6.13, each of the two-story dwellings faces south and toward the street with a generous walled courtyard in front. Deciduous trees shade the house and courtyard from the strong summer sun yet let the full sun of winter warm the house. The walls are built high not only for privacy but to keep whatever untidiness there is behind the gate. Although monotony of materials and overall layout is apparent, there is an orderliness and quiet that is reminiscent of traditional courtyard houses.

With the intent of assisting rural reconstruction, a nationwide competition was held in 1980 and 1981 to spur the design of rural dwellings. More than 6,500 detailed plans were submitted by professional architects, rural craftsmen, and others. Designers were to be concerned with the positive aspects of local architectural traditions, the provision of living space alongside the needs of subsidiary sideline production, the improve-

ment of spatial layout, and the need to economize on the use of space (Zhongguo jianzhu kexue 1982, x). Peasants were invited to comment on the designs and models. In June 1981, some 142 designs of the 6,500 submissions were selected as outstanding. Most of those selected were designed by individuals rather than professionals in design institutes. To popularize the plans, ninety-three were reproduced in a book to be sold in rural areas (Zhongguo jianzhu kexue 1982). Some of the designs have been promoted by architects who personally have traveled into the countryside to

Figure 6.13. Located in Qiliying, Henan province, these two-story structures are lined *en echelon* facing south. Built of brick and concrete, each includes a walled front courtyard.

speak with local people about the possibilities of the new designs.

The two First Prize designs represent plans for use in the north and in the south, each incorporating elements of traditional design with modern principles and materials (Figures 6.14 and 6.15). Each is conceived as a cell which can stand alone or be linked in series to form row housing. Some thought has been given to variations in the basic designs to allow for flexible use and to counter the monotony of repeating a common design in a given area. Both designs separate the kitchen from the living room *(tangwu)*, locating it according to different requirements in the north and south. The designs incorporate room for raising pigs and chickens and installation of a biogas converter. Although designed to accommodate a small nuclear family, each can satisfactorily house a second generation. These two designs, as we shall see, epitomize current developments in rural housing.

The North China Design

The design chosen for use in northern China, shown in Figure 6.14, comprises a basic plan with two variations, one a reverse plan of the house and the other with the courtyard in back rather than in front. The walled compound encompasses 217.15 square meters; the building area itself covers only 70.64 square meters of the total. Designed by a team from Tianjin, a large city on the north China plain to the east of Beijing, the layout is that of a single-story dwelling composed of a traditional three-bay *(jian)* rectangular unit. Nonetheless, the three-*jian* layout does not follow the traditional "one bright, two dark" *(yiming liangcn)* arrangement with the joint kitchen, common room, and storage area (the "one bright") in the middle with two flanking bedrooms (the "two dark"). Rather, carefully considered design

changes introduce an integrated yet separate kitchen in order to facilitate internal flow and provide greater privacy.

Separate entrances give access to the living room *(tangwu)* and kitchen *(chufang)* from the courtyard, a deviation from the common pattern. Adjacent to the kitchen stove in the selected model is a bedroom with a *kang* brick bed along the windowed southern wall, from which, according to the designers, "one's aged parents *(lauren)* can sit and watch the traditional activities in the courtyard." The other bedroom, the designers continue, "is flexibly laid out to meet the needs of new-style furniture and is designed without a *kang* bed, using a heater for warmth." Each of the two bedrooms averages 15 square meters in size, very generous especially in comparison with those currently found in city apartments. Both bedrooms break with tradition and include windows in the front and back for cross ventilation. This arrangement represents an improvement during summer, but caution must be taken in winter to insulate against the strong north and northwest winds. As an alternative in summer to using the stove connected to the *kang,* a methane gas hot plate is included in the kitchen.

With a recommended north/south orientation, the design incorporates a large south-facing courtyard in the front as well as a small open space in the back. In the basic model, as shown in the perspective and plane drawings, the front courtyard occupies more than fifty percent of the total area. It is less a space for leisure activities than one for carrying out subsidiary rural production. More than half the courtyard is intended for a large kitchen garden; the remainder is divided between a paved patio and walkway, a storage building and attached toilet, and a pigsty and chicken coop below which is the biogas converter *(zhaoqichi)* to produce methane for cooking and lighting. A

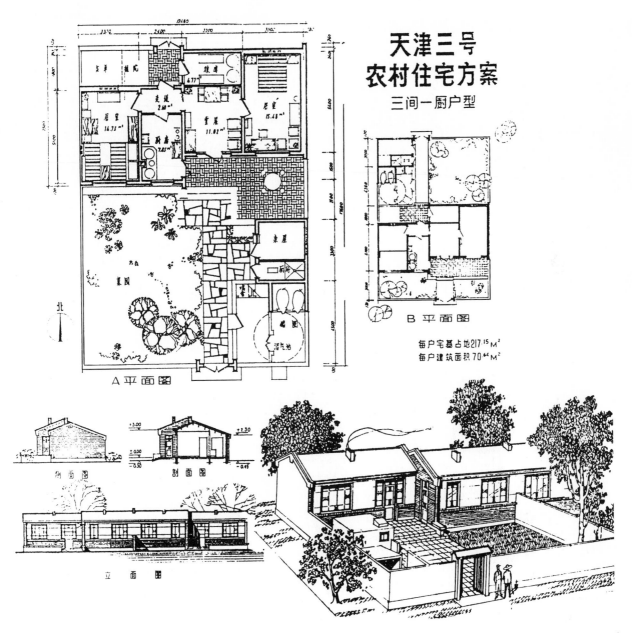

Figure 6.14. First Prize design for a modern dwelling for rural north China. Known as Tianjin Number 3, this single-story dwelling includes three *jian* and a kitchen. Plan A has the pigsty and latrine in front adjacent to the kitchen garden; Plan B places them in the rear, giving only a small open space in front.

四川一号

方案包括三个单元，二～四室户型，可组成二十余种组合体，适合2～8口人居住。平面布置较美，各户型居室大中小搭配，至不穿衩，楼上楼下房间，既既各目一致生活安静，住宅中部多功能庭厅，可民会客、或友、家务劳动及生产、卫生条件。居室与厨、厕之间有敞厅和小天井分隔，通风良好，减少煤气污染，改善了卫生条件。南厅内有明手明手暗的楼梯，联系方便。较好地反映了南方地区特有的民居风貌。

立面造型简朴大方，具有浓郁的农村风味，砖墙用料、砖坡，将砖用钢应力周筋混凝土空心板，屋面为小青瓦或干摆瓦等，构件统一，施工简便，便于村民们建，并可根据不同地形和住产变好，给个地建筑组合灵活。

甲、乙、丙单元建筑面积分别为115.87 M²、95.49 M²及76.61 M²。

鸟瞰图

底层平面图　二层平面图
底层平面图　二层平面图
底层平面图　二层平面图

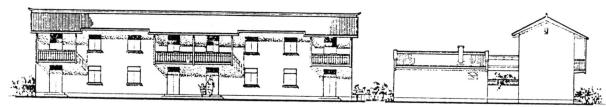

Figure 6.15. First Prize design for a modern dwelling for rural south China. Known as Sichuan Number 1, this duplex has a two-story living area joined to a single-story building containing the kitchen, storage area, bathing facilities, and pigpen. The two joined dwellings form a *sanheyuan*. Alternative layouts are shown. The plans include covered open spaces.

small rear courtyard abuts a storage area for firewood. Opposite is a 4.77-square-meter dry storage area for grain, an important consideration in a collective economy where as much as 300 kilograms of grain per capita may be distributed each year. Plan B shifts the large courtyard to the back of the house, unfortunately leaving it in shade during much of the winter. On the other hand, the rear courtyards allow the front of the houses to assume a more ordered appearance.

The winning design is to be built with locally fired clay bricks (zhantuzhuan). Wood is used only in the framing of windows and doors and, if available, may be used for the roof purlins. Dimensions are provided for the substitution of reinforced concrete purlins. Local practices can govern the makeup of the roof, using either a waterproof compound laid atop reed or wheat stalks or clay tiles set in a mud and grass composition. The front elevation carries forth the horizontal line characteristic of traditional rural dwellings in north China.

After the Tianjin Number 3 design was selected as the model for new dwellings in north China, the design team received inquiries from provinces throughout the north and northeast as well as Jiangxi in central China for detailed information. To meet this demand, a booklet was prepared showing three variants of the winning design as well as plans for four other single-story dwellings (pingfang) and four plans for two-story houses (loufang). (See Liu and Zhu 1983.) Using these and derivative plans, massive rural construction took place during 1984 on the rural outskirts of Tianjin; as a result nearly 300,000 rural families were able to move into "specially designed and built houses" on the eve of the 1985 Spring Festival. Also completed were a number of two-story villa-type "show houses" with changes which break down the traditional overlapping usage of

rooms. Each of these houses included separate rooms for dining, cooking, sleeping, bathing, and general family use. Moreover, the *China Daily* reported, "the courtyards have lawns and gardens with stone benches along paved paths" ("Tianjin" 1985).

The South China Design

The winning design for use in southern China, designated Sichuan Number 1, includes three variations of similar two-story units as shown in Figure 6.15. Since they can be joined together in more than twenty different arrangements to meet local conditions, they present a less monotonous layout than a single plan would provide. The designs incorporate two to four rooms, excluding the detached kitchen and an outside covered hall (changting) to accommodate households of from two to eight persons. The larger model covers 116.64 square meters, 100 square meters less than the north China model. Nonetheless, because of two-story construction, the enclosed living space is almost forty percent greater. All models have a living room, outside hall, and detached kitchen but differ in the number of bedrooms. Model A has three bedrooms, Model B two, and Model C one. Model C can occupy as little as 78 square meters of building space.

Several design features of the plans are especially suitable to the warm and humid conditions found through most of the year in southern China. Cross ventilation is provided in each room. The lower rooms are shaded from the sun by the roof of the outside covered hall; the roof itself serves as a veranda (shaitai) for the bedrooms on the second floor. Moreover, one bedroom has its own rear balcony. The detached kitchen keeps heat away from the living quarters. Between the kitchen and the house structure itself is the outside covered hall (changting) occupying 10.75

square meters in Model A and less area in the other two models. This shaded and well-ventilated court extends the living space outside, serving as a place to eat and entertain during the hot season. Extensive roof overhangs shade the windows from sun and rain.

Like the courtyards in the northern models, these southern designs include not only a large kitchen garden but also a pigsty and chicken coop. Set between the front gate and the pigsty is the toilet, both connected to a biogas converter for methane production. No separate space has been set aside for the storage of grain. The year-round growing season enjoyed in many southern parts of the country makes it less necessary to store large quantities of grain and other produce than in the colder north.

Sichuan Number 1 is designed to be built of brick, stone, or preformed concrete slabs according to local conditions. The roof too is adaptable to local materials. The designers describe the area encompassing the dwelling, outside covered hall, and small open court as "a simple and unadorned large square displaying a rural flavor" (Zhongguo jianzhu kexue 1982, 3).

Other Designs

The other 140 winning designs not only offer plans for traditional Han dwellings but present plans for the improvement of national minority dwellings as well, including a plan for the improvement of the Mongol yurt. Reflecting the differing amounts of land available for building sites, the plans range widely in the amount of space they occupy, from more than 100 square meters to nearly 300. Some plans, such as Zhejiang Number 1, occupy only 117.92 square meters of land yet can accommodate three generations of six to eight people in four bedrooms (Zhongguo jianzhu kexue 1982, 25). None of the

plans, however, seems to meet the restrictive limit of 75 square meters of building space imposed in Magang brigade in Shunde *xian* of Guangdong province, where two, three, and even four-story dwellings have been built in recent years to overcome the miniscule land parcels available (Feng 1983, 51–52).

The winning rural housing designs promise a minimum of 6 square meters per person; most plans exceed 9 square meters. The compact two-storied Shanxi Number 1 design provides 12.1 square meters per person. Current figures for urban housing, by comparison, range only between 4 and 6 square meters per person with expectations of exceeding 8 square meters by the year 2000. Figures 6.16 and 6.17 show a representative selection of the housing designs chosen in the national competition.

ENERGY REQUIREMENTS AND SOLAR HOUSING

Energy sources in China's countryside are at once in serious short supply and astonishingly wasted. Drawing on the organic materials about them, Chinese peasants consume enormous volumes of firewood and brush for cooking purposes and for winter warmth. Unless easily available locally, coal is normally difficult to obtain and expensive. Neither natural gas nor kerosine use is significant. Consumption of biomass fuels such as crop residues, wood, and grasses has been increasing, moreover, as household subsidiary production expands, contributing further to the depletion of soil fertility and the destruction of woodlands in the quest for energy. It is estimated that approximately 70 million rural households (forty percent of the total) do not have access to electricity and that "most villages had to go without fuel for two months every year" (Liu Dizhong 1984, 1). State

Figure 6.16. A selection of winning designs for use in north China. *Top:* Shanxi Number 1, either freestanding or with an enclosed utility courtyard in front. *Center:* Hebei Number 4, traditional three-*jian* arrangement with fronting courtyard. *Bottom:* Hebei Number 1, built for lateral and vertical growth.

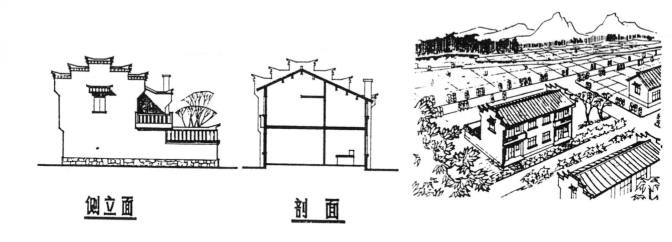

側立面 剖 面

Figure 6.17. A selection of winning designs for use in south China. *Top:* Zhejiang Number 1, designed with traditional stepped gables, to house three generations. *Bottom:* Anhui Number 2, a compact two-story dwelling suitable for rugged terrain.

planners have begun to examine these factors in an effort to improve the use of conventional energy sources and popularize the use of less common methods. Biogas conversion as well as solar, tidal, and wind sources of energy are all being explored.

China has a long and continuing history that reaches to neolithic times of siting dwellings in optimal relation to the sun in order to maximize natural light and heat. Chinese architects and vernacular builders persist in their concern for proper siting to benefit from the seasonal movement of the sun's path across the sky. Recently a more scientific approach has been taken in order to maximize favorable solar conditions. Calculations have established the best orientation for dwellings in most provinces, confirming traditional preferences yet generally expanding their ranges (Jilinsheng 1979, 124–125). Prototypes of active solar rural housing have been built across the country. Prominent are those built in the so-called solar village of Yihezhuang, Daxing *xian,* to the south of Beijing. Experimental designs have been built there to measure their comparative effectiveness (Figures 6.18 and 6.19). Several prototypes of successful European suburban houses have been built that, except for orientation, strikingly break with traditional Chinese house design (Figure 6.20). Nearby in the prosperous village of Liuminying, passive solar housing developed by architects at Qinghua University is under construction (Figure 6.21). Other schools of architecture

Figure 6.18. Single-story multiple-*jian* dwelling with passive solar collectors in Yihezhuang, southern suburbs of Beijing.

Figure 6.19. Two-story passive solar design at "Solar Village," Yihezhuang. The occupants utilize a solar stove.

elsewhere in the country are carrying out similar experimental enterprises.

Moreover, efforts are under way to expand the variety of sources for cooking and small-scale industrial uses of alternative energy sources. Energy-saving stoves that improve the efficiency of burning wood and straw have appeared in rural areas around Beijing; some 260,000 units were installed in 1984 ("Farmers" 1985, 3). It has been estimated that the common brick stove found in traditional dwellings provides only ten to fifteen percent of the potential heat available from the materials burned (Liu Dizhong 1984, 1). The improvement of the efficiency of the common stove would not only conserve the already limited fuel supplies, it would also contribute to a lessening of the pressure on the fragile rural ecosystem resulting from the rapacious quest for fuel. In addition, 40,000 solar stoves like the one shown in Figure 6.19 have been built experimentally in the country but have only limited utility at present. Solar water heaters now rise above dwellings in the suburbs of some major cities.

Utilizing human waste, animal manure, stubble, and other organic material, biogas conversion pits (zhaoqichi) have been in use in the country for more than a decade. The Chinese admit that a high proportion of these early anaerobic digesters failed to meet minimal specification and thus proved inefficient. Since 1979, in an attempt to convince rural households of the value of biogas conversion pits as decentralized energy sources, cautious efforts have been made to repair those that could be salvaged while those that could not be made functional were abandoned. Furthermore, biogas conversion pits are being retrofitted into some existing houses and designed into new housing, as in the Tianjin Number 3 design discussed above.

Providing energy mainly for summertime cooking and nighttime lighting, approximately 4 million biogas converters, serving perhaps 20 million peasants, have been installed in the countryside. Found mainly in the southeast and southwest areas of the country where higher temperatures increase their efficiency, there are plans for 10 million more by 1990 ("Biogas" 1984, 3). One

authority optimistically predicts that as much as five percent of rural household energy will be supplied as biogas by 1990 (Kharbanda and Qureshi 1985, 3). They are, as a critical observer of environmental degradation in China has pointed out, "a clever multiple solution to problems of energy supply, crop fertilization and environmental hygiene" and are likely to play an increasing role in alleviating rural energy shortages (Smil 1984, 152–153).

As many as sixty percent of Chinese rural households are connected to a power source that gives the convenience of a light at night or, more recently, the use of a television set. The per capita consumption of all electric power in rural China in 1980, however, was less than 40 kwh per year, an amount sufficient only to light one 50-watt

Figure 6.20. Active solar houses of European design at Yihezhuang. Except for the use of brick and a southern orientation, the structure differs from a common Chinese house in layout and style.

Figure 6.21. Model of a passive solar rural duplex designed by the Department of Architecture, Qinghua University. This design is under construction at Liuminying, a prosperous village in Daxing *xian,* south of Beijing.

bulb per person two hours per day during the year (Smil 1984, 149). Large and small hydroelectric generating facilities and biogas conversion pits serve as the principal source of this power. Overall rural residential energy requirements are likely to increase not only in response to changing domestic patterns of usage but also stimulated by subsidiary production that takes the dwelling as its locus.

CURRENT BUILDING MATERIALS AND PROBLEMS

Tamped earth, adobe, fired bricks, stone, wood—all have been used as traditional building materials in rural China. As economic conditions improved in the past, peasants typically repaired walls or built new houses using fired bricks instead of the cheaper tamped earth and adobe bricks. Such practices have continued to the present both in urban and rural construction to the degree that about 154 billion clay bricks were produced in 1980 alone to meet the demand (*China Handbook* 1984, 169). The years since have seen even a greater volume of brick manufacture, a good deal of it consuming arable land to support the demand in cities for building materials. In some areas, cemeteries have come to serve as borrow areas for soil for brick making, leaving many burial areas pockmarked centers of great activity (Figure 6.22). According to reports, even important archaeological sites, such as the A Fang Palace at Xianyang near Xian, which dates back to the Qin dynasty, were being defaced by rural construction teams digging into the historically important podium to build kilns and form bricks ("Brick" 1985, 3).

Critics have estimated that with 15 million bricks dug from a single hectare of land, at least 100 hectares of land is being consumed each year in the making of bricks alone. The enlargement of dwellings, construction of new housing, as well as haphazard rural industrial expansion all have had an impact on cropland. It has been reported that new rural housing alone accounted for fully two-fifths of all cropland taken out of cultivation between 1957 and 1978 (Smil 1984, 72). Pressures have increased further in recent years and account in some degree for the increased popularity of multiple-story dwellings that meet rural household demands for greater space in a socially and environmentally responsible way.

Some have called for the development of alternative building materials (Li 1982). Progress has been made in the development of light concrete blocks as well as prefabricated reinforced concrete panels, beams, and pillars. The use of layered

Figure 6.22. In the quest for soil to make bricks, cemeteries have become active areas for brickmaking. Near Guilin, Guangxi Zhuang Autonomous Region.

compound boards of cement, gypsum, and felt has increased. In some areas, the casting of reinforced concrete columns or walls takes place at the construction site using aerocrete (Figure 6.23). Except for the casting of walls on site, these building materials can be produced in factories which draw either on local raw materials or those brought from other areas. There has been notable success in recent years in the use of these alternative materials in the construction of urban multistoried buildings and in public buildings in rural areas. Although China's cement output is enormous and production occurs in small plants all over the country, there have nevertheless been major shortfalls in the availability of cement even

with the seventy-one percent production increase to 80 million tons between 1976 and 1980 (Lin, Zhou, and Qi 1984, 287–288).

Peasants nonetheless persevere in preferring locally produced brick, the availability of which can be governed by local authorities drawing upon local resources. Attention continues to be focused on the source of the local clay in an attempt to reduce the impact on farmland, some even claiming that "land saving is as important as family planning" (Wang 1984, 50). A further problem has resulted from the fact that the firing of bricks in common small kilns that have come to dot the countryside now consumes "an appalling amount of coal—nearly 20 million tons every

Figure 6.23. Where wood columns are in short supply, reinforced concrete pillars are being substituted. Daxing *xian,* Beijing municipality.

year, almost half of the total consumed by the building materials industry" (*China Handbook* 1984, 169). The gap between supply and demand as well as the enormous depletion of raw materials because of massive construction present major obstacles to the growth of new housing. Large brick kilns that benefit from economies of scale have been built to meet swelling demand and reduce the ravaging of arable land by individual and collective brickmakers (Figure 6.24).

Apart from problems in the production and supply of cement and bricks for the improvement of rural dwellings, there are shortages of wood and window glass as well. Timber continues to be in short supply in most areas of China, a fact that is inconsistent with the many reports of extensive afforestation carried out over the past thirty-five years. Recent evidence, however, reveals a stag-

gering amount of deforestation in the country because of legal and illegal cutting and, most significantly, low regeneration rates of new growth. The resulting problems are acute and are being addressed in order to retard the destructive overall environmental consequences (Smil 1984, 9–37). Trees appropriate for construction purposes such as for pillars, purlins, and rafters are being specifically planted as shown in Figure 6.25. These renewable woodlots also provide organic material to feed pigs and fuel stoves. Shortages especially exist in north China; greater variety and amounts of timber are available in the northeast, southeast, and southwest. Bamboo is widely used south of the Changjiang (Yangzi) River. The availability of window glass has been described as acute; in fact annual production meets only forty percent of the current demand (*China Handbook* 1984, 167).

Peasants have experimented with the use of wall tiles, terrazzo floors, and even wallpaper to supplement traditional materials and improve maintenance, yet their use is not widespread because of limited supply.

Recognizing the negative impact of urban and rural housing construction on farmland as well as the chronic shortages of alternative building materials that could curb the tendency to plunder arable land for short-term gain, efforts are being made to find remedies. In Beijing, the China Rural Housing Building Materials Company has been formed to work with rural housing corporations throughout the country to supply essential building materials in a planned way. Using loans from the Construction Bank of China and other lending institutions, they propose to produce and distribute steel, cement, and glass to help meet the burgeoning demand ("Rural Construction" 1985).

SUMMARY

The full scope of rural housing improvement cannot be determined since China's capital construction investment statistics do not include the sums

Figure 6.24. Benefiting from economies of scale, many large partially mechanized brick kilns have been built to meet the needs of urban and rural areas. Dunhuang, Gansu province.

Figure 6.25. Woodlots have been planted in many rural areas to help meet the demand for wood for pillars, purlins, and rafters. Fenghuo, Shaanxi province.

spent in the building of houses by individuals or collectives. Yet it is clear that peasants have been guided by current policy to channel their rapidly increasing incomes into housing stock. The pace of construction has moved to overcome the neglect of many decades, time during which the country's rural population itself doubled. The task and the problems are enormous. Although the state retains the major responsibility for re-building and rehabilitating housing in the crowded urban areas where self-help is less possible, it is clear that the principal efforts at revitalizing rural housing stock will continue to come largely from the rural population itself.

Conferences, competitions, and publications increasingly focus on assisting the rural population in planning, designing, and building houses in China's countryside. Two significant publications appeared in 1984 to promote the orderly development of housing rehabilitation and construction. The 900-page *Handbook of Rural Building,* with more than 64,000 copies in print, is likely to have a significant impact on improving and standardizing the various approaches to rural planning and construction across the country. There is substantial concern for the improvement of sanitary conditions and the provision of space for subsidiary production.

The editors warn that readers must "guard against indiscriminately copying" ideas presented in the handbook (Jiang et al. 1984, 3). Nonetheless, it is possible that the handbook will be seen in the rural areas as a blueprint for modernization and therefore, perhaps unconsciously, set limits on the forms that rural building will take. On the other hand, those who come in contact with the handbook may well be challenged to integrate local realities with the technological ideas presented. Architects and builders have proved and peasants have accepted the use of reinforced concrete posts and beams where wood once was used exclusively—a compelling necessity in a country still plagued by a shortage of building timber. Fitting houses to natural conditions, especially the seasonal passage of the sun, enhances the use of an important energy source for heating and drying. Unfortunately, the concentration of large numbers of dwellings following a common orientation and the tendency to follow available pattern books is imposing a monotonous rhythm on the countryside.

To spur the systematic improvement of rural China, the State Council issued a volume titled *Research Materials for the Construction of Rural Houses* (Guowuyuan 1984). This small volume includes all the important documents relating to rural housing issued since 1979. Prepared for the use of local cadres in informing peasants of areas of governmental concern and proscription, the booklet aims to counter the common tendency of peasants to regard house construction as a matter to be conducted without governmental guidance. The need for land-use planning as well as the rational and legal use of building materials are compelling elements in the effort to bring an ordered development to China's countryside and to improve significantly the quality of China's rural housing stock.

Chinese planners and peasant builders, as they move toward the provision of rural housing with more space, air, and light and better sanitation, are confronted with the need to acknowledge and improve upon the inherited building tradition. Using technology to overcome shortages of certain building materials, new rural houses continue to resonate traditional patterns. Dramatic increases in rural income levels in recent years are expected to continue to find expression in new housing construction. Yet governed as housing also is by internal forces, future rural housing forms no doubt will reflect not only the evolving modifications in the composition of the Chinese family but also the changes taking place in China's rural labor force as surplus rural labor, instead of migrating to cities, leaves the land but not the village *(li tu buli cun)*. These changes, as some Chinese planners, officials, and outside observers now see them, will shift large proportions of peasants from agriculture to rural industry and commerce over the next two decades with a resulting transformation of the settlement landscape of the countryside.

GLOSSARY OF CHINESE TERMS

ang	昂	cantilever		*daixue*	袋穴	pit dwellings
an men	安门	to install a door		*dangwa*	当瓦	roof tile
aoting yaodong	凹庭窑洞	sunken-courtyard cave dwelling		*dankaijian*	单开间	house about 10 *chi* wide
				daocao	稻草	rice straw
				dating	大厅	main hall of a house
bagua	八卦	Eight Trigrams		*difang zhi*	地方志	local gazetteer
banxueju	半穴居	semisubterranean dwelling		*diyao*	地窑	sunken-courtyard cave dwelling
bieye	别墅	country villa				
				dong	栋	ridgepole
cai buwailu	财不外露	to stop the wealth from leaving		*dong tu*	动土	to break ground for a house
				dougong	斗拱	eaves brackets
changting	敞厅	outside covered hall		*duilian*	对联	couplets
chao	巢	tree hut				
cheng	城	city wall; city				
chengzhong	承重墙	load-bearing		*erfang*	二房	"second room"; bedroom for the second generation
chi	尺	a unit of length; $\frac{1}{3}$ meter				
chiwei	鸱尾	"owl's tail" roof profile, modified in Taiwan as the *yanwei* style				
				fengshui	风水	geomancy ("wind and water")
chuandou	穿斗	pillars and transverse tie beams		*fengshui shi*	风水师	geomancer ("wind and water interpreter")
chuanfang	穿枋	transverse tie beam		*fengshui xian-sheng*	风水先生	geomancer ("wind and water interpreter")
chuantiao	椽条	purlin		*fenjia*	分家	to divide a family
chuanzi	椽子	beam rafter		*fenqiang*	粉墙	whitewashed walls
chufang	厨房	cooking area; kitchen		*fu*	福	happiness
cizhu	刺竹	thorny bamboo				
cukangtu	粗糠土	plaster of mud and rice chaff		*gaoliang gan*	高粱秆	kaoliang stalks
cuo	厝	shelter		*gelou*	阁楼	loft
				gongting	公厅	central room, main hall
dafang	大房	"great room"; bedroom for the senior generation		*guazhu*	瓜柱	short queen post, strut

hangtu	夯土	tamped earth		*loufang*	楼房	multistory building
hengtiao	横条	purlin		*Lu Ban chi*	鲁班尺	carpenter's rule
hongwa	红瓦	red roof tiles		*luoban*	罗盘	geomancer's instrument
hongzhuan	红砖	red bricks		*luwei*	芦苇	reeds for thatching
huangtu	黄土	loessial soil		*luxi*	芦席	reed mat for roofing
hucuo	护厝	side halls of a Fujian dwelling (equivalent to *xiangfang* and *pixie*)		*mabei*	马背	horseback or saddle roof
				maijie	麦秸	wheat straw
huijiang	灰浆	mortar		*maijieni*	麦秸泥	wheat-straw plaster
huini	灰泥	plaster		*manzu*	蛮族	southern barbarian
huizhuan	灰砖	gray bricks		*maocao*	茅草	thatching
hulong	护龙	"protector dragons"; side halls of a dwelling		*maoci*	茅茨	thatch (classical usage)
				maolu	茅庐	thatched cottage
hunningtu	混凝土	concrete		*maoshe*	茅舍	thatched cottage
				maowu	茅屋	thatched cottage
jia	家	family		*meizha*	煤渣	cinders
jian	间	area between four pillars; unit of measure; a bay		*men*	门	door, gate
				menshen	门神	door gods
jiaqi	家气	family spirit		*miliang pingding*	密梁平顶	pillar-and-purlin construction
jichu	基础	tamped foundation or base		*mingqi*	明器	funerary objects
jilin	脊檩	ridgepole		*mu*	亩	area measurement (0.066 hectare)
jin	进	one of several rows of a dwelling within an old-style courtyard				
				mugoujia jiegou	木构架结构	wood frame construction
jinggan	井干	log dwelling		*muyao*	木妖	"wooden magic"
kaijian	开间	the standard width of a room in an old-style house (about 10 *chi*, the length of a purlin); a bay		*neihu*	内户	initial pair of *hulong*
				niantu zhuan	粘土砖	clay bricks
				niaozhuan	鸟砖	gray bricks from Fujian
				pi	坯	brick
kang	炕	brick bed with internal flues		*pingfang*	平房	single-story dwelling
kaoshan yaodong	靠山窑洞	cliffside caves		*pingwu*	平屋	single-story dwelling
kenzhao	垦照	land patent		*pixie*	僻榭	side halls of Fujian dwellings
keting	客厅	central room, main hall				
konghanzhu	空涵竹	lengthy bamboo used for building		*qi*	气	family spirit; also *jiaqi*
				qianggen	墙根	foundation of a wall
li	里	approximately ⅓ mile		*qiangzhu goujia*	墙柱构架	wall-and-post structure
li tu buli cun	离土不离村	"to leave the land but not the village"		*qiantang houqin*	前堂后寝	front hall and back bedrooms
				qiantang houshi	前堂后室	front hall and back bedrooms
liang	梁	beam		*qiqiang*	砌墙	to lay bricks; build a wall
liangzhu	梁柱	pillar-and-beam construction		*qijushi*	起居室	living room
liao	寮	hut		*qinghui*	青灰	mortar
lin	檩	purlin		*qinghui wa*	青灰瓦	half-burnt tiles
lintiao	檩条	purlin		*quchi*	曲尺	carpenter's square
linzi	檩子	purlin				
liqiang	篱墙	wattled wall		*sanheyuan*	三合院	courtyard-style dwelling with no rooms at the gate

sanjianqi	三间起	three-bay dwelling
sha	砂	contours of the earth recognized in *fengshui*
shaitai	晒台	veranda; flat roof
shangliang	上梁	to raise the principal roof beam
shanqiang	上墙	gable end of dwelling, ("mountain wall")
shantouqiang	山头墙	same as *shanqiang*
she	社	settlement
shi gandang	石敢当	"the stone dares to resist"
shihui	石灰	lime
shuangkaijian	双开间	a house about 10 *chi* wide
siheyuan	四合院	Beijing-style courtyard house with buildings on four sides
siwuding	四庑顶	hipped roof
sizhuding	四注顶	hipped roof
tailiang	台梁	pillar-and-beam construction
tangwu	堂屋	central room of a traditional Chinese house
teng	藤	rattan
tianjing	天井	"skywell"; small courtyard
tianjingyuan yaodong	天井院窑洞	courtyard-style cave complex
tingjing	厅井	linking of the main hall (*tingtang*) and courtyard (*tingyuan*) as unified space, especially in Fujian
tingtang	厅堂	main hall in Fujian (faces the *tingyuan*)
tingyuan	庭院	courtyard of Fujian dwelling (faces the *tingtang*)
tongwa	筒瓦	roof tiles in a bamboo shape
tujiao	土角	clay bricks; unburnt bricks
tu lou	土楼	circular dwelling in southeast construction
tumu	土木	
tu pi	土坯	clay bricks; unburnt brick
wadang	瓦当	eaves tiles; tile ends
waihu	外护	second pair of *hulong*
waiwaihu	外外护	third pair of *hulong*
wangban	望板	roof boards
wapian	瓦片	tile wall covering
wengong		carpenter's rule
wo	窝	hut

wudianding	庑殿顶	hipped roof; see also *sizhuding*
wuding	屋顶	roof
wufu linmen	五福临门	"five blessings knocking on the door"
wuji	屋脊	ridge of a roof
wujia	屋架	roof truss
wuyan	屋檐	eaves
wuyu	屋宇	house
xian	县	county
xiangfang	相房	side halls of a dwelling
xiangfang	相方	to examine the aspects of a site for a residence
xiaomi gan	小米干	millet stalks for thatching
xieshanding	歇山顶	combined gable and hipped roof
xincun	新村	new-style village
xuanshanding	悬山顶	"overhanging gables" roof style
xue	穴	building site; literally "the dragon's lair"
yamen	衙门	administrative headquarters
yang	阳	male or positive principle in nature; the sun; the southerly direction
yangfang	洋房	"foreign building"; a two-story dwelling
yanwei	燕尾	swallowtail-style roof profile
yanzi	檐子	eaves
yaodong	窑洞	cave dwelling
yecao	野草	wild grasses
yi	邑	settlement
yijin huanxiang	衣锦还乡	"return to one's hometown in silken robes"; return after making good
yiming liangan	一明两暗	"one bright, two dark"; north China house type
yin	阴	female or negative principle in nature; the northerly direction
yingbi	影壁	screen wall facing the inside or outside of a gate of a courtyard; see also *zhaobi*
yingshanding	硬山顶	"firm mountain" roof style with no roof overhanging the gables

yingshanjialin	硬山架檁	gable wall with purlin framework
yuan lou	圆楼	circular dwelling in southeast
yuanluo	院落	courtyard
zhantuzhuan	粘土砖	claybricks
zhaobi	照壁	spirit wall, also called *yingbi*
zhaoqichi	沼汽池	biogas converter pit
zhengshen	正身	main section of a dwelling
zhengting	正厅	main hall, central room

zhu	柱	pillar, post
zhuang	幢	a measure for buildings
zhuanpi	砖坯	unfired bricks
zhuanyao	砖窑	brick kiln
zhuchu	柱础	pedestal, plinth, base
zhuzuo	柱座	pedestal, plinth, base
zuobei chaonan	座北朝南	back toward the north, face toward the south
zuo zao	作灶	to build a stove

REFERENCES CITED

Baker, Hugh D. R.
  1979 *Ancestral Images: A Hong Kong Album.* Hong Kong: South China Morning Post.

Banpo yizhi [Banpo Site Museum]
  1982 Xian: Renmin chubanshe.

Beazeley, M.
  1885 "Notes on an Overland Journey Through the Southern Part of Formosa." *Proceedings, Royal Geographical Society and Monthly Record of Geography,* n.s. 7:1–23.

Beijing shi dier fangwu xiushan gongcheng gongsi gujianke yanjiu sheji shi [The Number Two Dwellings Renovation Construction Company of Beijing, Ancient Architectural Techniques Research Unit]
  1983 "Gu jianzhu zhuanliao ji jiagong jishu" [Bricks and bricklaying techniques in ancient building]. *Gujian yuanlin jishu* [The techniques of ancient building of gardens] 1:21–27.

Beijing shi jianshe shejiyuan, nongcun zhuzhai shejizu [Rural Houses Design Group, Beijing Building Design Institute]
  1962 "Miyun xinjian nongcun juzhai diaocha" [Investigation of new rural construction in Miyun]. *Jianzhu xuebao* [Architectural journal] 10:3–10.

Bennett, Steven J.
  1978 "Patterns of Sky and Earth: A Chinese System of Applied Cosmology." *Chinese Science* 3:1–26.

"Biogas to Substitute for Coal, Firewood"
  1984 *China Daily* 4 (955): 3. August 17.

Boyd, Andrew
  1962 *Chinese Architecture and Town Planning: 1500 B.C.–A.D. 1911.* Chicago: University of Chicago Press.

Braudel, Fernand
  1979 *The Structures of Everyday Life: Civilization and Capitalism: 15th–18th Century.* New York: Harper & Row.

"Brick Kilns Damage Aged Palace Ruins"
  1985 *China Daily* 4 (1109): 3. February 15.

Buck, John Lossing
  1937 *Land Utilization in China.* Chicago: University of Chicago Press.

Burkhardt, V. R.
  1955 *Chinese Creeds and Customs.* Vol. 2. Hong Kong: South China Morning Post.

Campbell, William
  1903 *Formosa Under the Dutch: Described from Contemporary Records.* London: Kegan Paul, Trench, Trubner & Co.

Chang, Kwang-chih
  1976 *Early Chinese Civilization: Anthropological Perspectives.* Cambridge: Harvard University Press.
  1980 *Shang Civilization.* New Haven: Yale University Press.

Chen Fanghui [Chen Fang-hoei]
  1968 "Taiwan chubu Urasato no haitaku to shuraku" [The pioneer settlement of the Puli basin]. *Jimbun chiri* [Human geography] 20:322–329.

Chen Nainieh, trans.
1960   "Taibei pendi minzu nongjia fangwu zhi gou-
        zao yu shebei" [The materials and building of
        rural farmhouses by Fujian settlers in the Tai-
        bei basin]. *Taibei wenwu* [Cultural relics of Tai-
        bei] 8:103–123.

Cheng Jiyue and Hu Chengen
1980   "Shexian Mingdai juzhu jianzhu 'lao wujiao
        (ge)' diaocha jianbao" [Brief report on the
        Ming dynasty houses "Lau Wu Guo" in She-
        xian]. *Jianzhu lishi yu lilun* [Corpus of architec-
        tural history and theory] 1:104–111.

China Handbook Editorial Committee, compilers
1984   *China Handbook: Economy.* Beijing: Foreign Lan-
        guages Press.

Cohen, Myron L.
1970   "Developmental Process in the Chinese Do-
        mestic Group." In Maurice Freedman, ed.,
        Family and Kinship in Chinese Society, pp. 21–36.
        Stanford: Stanford University Press.
1976   *House United, House Divided: The Chinese Family
        in Taiwan.* New York: Columbia University
        Press.

"Constitution of the People's Republic of China"
1983   In *Fifth Session of the Fifth National People's Con-
        gress (Main Documents).* Beijing: Foreign Lan-
        guages Press.

"Construction Booms in Rural China"
1985   *China Daily* 4 (1204): 3. June 4.

Couling, Samuel
1917   *The Encyclopaedia Sinica.* Shanghai: Kelly &
        Walsh.

Dai Yanhui
1963   "Qingdai Taiwan xiangzhuang zhi jianli ji qi
        zuzhi" [The establishment and organization of
        rural settlements in Taiwan during the Qing
        period]. *Taiwan jingjishi, jiuji* [Economic history
        of Taiwan, no. 9]. Taibei: Taiwan yinhang.

de Groot, J. J. M.
1897   *The Religious System of China.* Leiden: E. J.
        Brill.

Deng Qisheng
1980   "Woguo gudai jianzhu wumian fangshui cuo-
        shi" [Measures adopted in building waterproof
        roofs in ancient China]. *Keji shi wenji* [Collec-
        tion on the history of science and technology]
        5:135–141.

Dillingham, Reed and Chang-lin Dillingham
1971   *Taiwan chuantong jianzhu zhi kaocha* [Survey of
        traditional architecture of Taiwan]. Taizhong:
        Donghai daxue.

Dixue tanyuan [An investigation into the origins of *fengshui*]
1966   Taibei: Liuyi chubanshe.

Dore, Henry
1917–   *Researches into Chinese Superstitions.* Shanghai:
1918   T'usewei Printing Press.

Eberhardt, Wolfgang
1965   *Folktales of China.* Chicago: University of Chi-
        cago Press.

Fang Jinggen and Chen Rinong
1980   "About Housing in China Today." *China Recon-
        structs* 29 (9): 11–12.

"Farmers Warm Up to Wood Stoves"
1985   *China Daily* 4 (1122): 3. February 28.

Fei Hsiao-tung [Fei Xiaotong]
1983   *Chinese Village Close-up.* Beijing: New World
        Press.

Feng Hua
1983   "Housing Boom in the Pearl River Delta."
        China Reconstructs 32 (10): 51–54.

Feuchtwang, Stephen
1974   *An Anthropological Analysis of Chinese Geomancy.*
        Vientiane: Vithagna.

"Flat Sales Cure Housing Headaches"
1985   *Beijing Review* 28 (25): 6–7. June 24.

Freedman, Maurice
1964   "Geomancy and Ancestor Worship." In *Chinese
        Lineage and Society: Fukien and Kwangtung,* pp.
        118–154. New York: Humanities Press.
1969   "Geomancy." In *Proceedings, Royal Anthropologi-
        cal Institute of Great Britain and Ireland, 1968,* pp.
        5–15. London: Royal Anthropological Insti-
        tute.

Fu Xinian
1984   "Survey: Chinese Traditional Architecture." In
        Nancy Shatzman Steinhardt, ed., *Chinese Tradi-
        tional Architecture,* pp. 9–33. New York: China
        Institute in America.

Gamble, Sidney D.
1954   *Ting Hsien: A North China Rural Community.* New
        York: Institute of Pacific Relations.

Gao Shangde and Zeng Hujiu, eds.
1982   *Xincun guihua* [The planning of new villages].
        Beijing: Zhongguo jianzhu gongye chubanshe.

Gao Zhenming, Yang Daoming, and Chen Yu
1983   "Fujian minju luejing" [A glance at rural

dwellings in Fujian]. *Jianzhu shi* [The architect] 16:143–161.

Glahn, Else
1981   "Chinese Building Standards in the Twelfth Century." *Scientific American* 244:162–173.
1982   "The Tradition of Chinese Building." In K. G. Izikowitz and P. Sorensen, eds., *The House in East and Southeast Asia*, pp. 25–34. Scandinavian Institute of Asian Studies Monograph Series no. 30. London: Curzon Press.
1984   "Unfolding the *Chinese Building Standards:* Research on the *Yingzao fashi*." In Nancy Shatzman Steinhardt, ed., *Chinese Traditional Architecture*, pp. 48–57. New York: China Institute in America.

Governor-General of Formosa
1928   *Taiwan Zaiseki Kanminzoku Gokan-betsu Chosa* [Investigation into the native places of the Han people of Taiwan]. Taihoku: Taiwan Sotoku Kanbu Chosa-ka.

Guan Huashan [Kwan Hua-san]
1980   "Taiwan chuantong minzhai suobiaoxian de kongjian guannian" [Traditional houses and folk space concepts in Taiwan]. *Zhongyang yanjiuyuan, minzuxue yanjiusuo jikan* [Journal of the Institute of Ethnology, Academia Sinica] 49:175–215.

Guang Jing Tang
1975   Hong Kong: Hanming xiongdi yinshuachang.

Guangzhou shi wenwu guanli weiyuanhui [Guangzhou Municipal Cultural Relics Administration], eds.
1958   *Guangzhou chutu Handai taowu* [Han dynasty pottery houses excavated in Guangzhou]. Beijing: Wenwu chubanshe.

Guo Husheng
1981   "Guanyu 'Lu Ban Yingzao Zhengshi' he 'Lu Ban Jing' " [The "Builders' Guide of Lu Ban" and the "Lu Ban Classic"]. *Keji shi wenji* [Collection on the history of science and technology] 7:98–105.

Guojia tongji ju [State Statistical Bureau]
1985   *Zhongguo tongji zhaiyao 1985* [China: a statistics survey in 1985]. Beijing: Xin shijie chubanshe.

Guowuyuan bangongting diaocha yanjiushi [Investigation and research office, State Council]
1984   *Nongfang jianshe yanjiu ziliao* [Research materials for the construction of rural houses]. Beijing: Zhongguo jianzhu gongye chubanshe.

Han Baode
1973   *Dougong de qiyuan yu fazhan* [The origin and development of the Chinese bracketing system]. Taibei: Wensheng shuju.

Han Baode and Hong Wenxiong
1973   *Banqiao Lin zhai: diaocha yanjiu ji xiufu jihua* [Banqiao Lin family compound: the survey, study, and restoration]. Taizhong: Donghai daxue.

He Kang
1985   "Zhongguo nongcun jingji tizhi gaige he nongye fazhan qianjing" [A perspective on the reform of China's rural economic system and agricultural development]. *Renmin ribao—haiwaiban* [People's daily—overseas edition] 2. November 13.

Ho, Ping-ti
1975   *The Cradle of the East: An Inquiry into the Indigenous Origins of Techniques and Ideas of Neolithic and Early Historic China, 5000–1000* B.C. Hong Kong: Chinese University of Hong Kong Press.

Hommel, Rudolf P.
1937   *China at Work*. New York: John Day.

Hou Jiyao
1982   "Shaanxi yaodong minju" [The cave dwellings of Shaanxi]. *Jianzhu xuebao* [Architectural journal] 10:71–73.

"Housing Reforms to End Inequities and Short Supply"
1985   *China Daily* 4 (1145): 4. March 27.

"Housing Survey"
1985   *China Daily* 5·(1233): 3. July 3.

Hsu Wen-hsiung
1975   "The Chinese Colonization of Formosa." Ph.D. dissertation, University of Chicago.
1980   "From Aboriginal Island to Chinese Frontier: The Development of Taiwan Before 1683." In Ronald G. Knapp, ed., *China's Island Frontier: Studies in the Historical Geography of Taiwan*, pp. 3-29. Honolulu: The University Press of Hawaii.

Huang Hanmin
1982   "Fujian minju de chuantong tese yu difang fengge" [The traditional character and local styles of the folk dwellings of Fujian]. Thesis, Qinghua University, Beijing.
1984   *Fujian minju de chuantong tese yu difang fenge, shang* [The traditional character and local styles of folk dwellings of Fujian: pt. 1]. *Jianzhushi* [The architect] 19:178–203.

Huang Yu-mei
1983   "A Home for All Seasons." *Free China Review* 34 (6): 35–41.

Jiang Zhengrong et al., eds.
1984   *Nongcun jianzhu shouce* [Handbook of rural building]. Beijing: Zhongguo jianzhu gongye chubanshe.

Jilinsheng jianzhu shejiyuan [Architectural Design Institute of Jilin Province]
1979   *Jianzhu rizhao sheji* [Design of solar architecture]. Beijing: Zhongguo jianzhu gongye chubanshe.

Jin Obo
1982   "Soil Technology." *Mimar: Architecture in Development* 3:48–53.

Jingdezhen buowuguan [Jingdezhen Museum]
1981   "Jingdezhen faxian dapi zhengui de Mingdai jianzhu" [Large group of rare structures of the Ming dynasty discovered in Jingdezhen]. *Jianzhu lishi yu lilun* [Corpus of architectural history and theory] 2:42.

Kharabanda, V. P. and M. A. Quereshi
1985   "Giants Compared: Biogas Applications Policy and Practice in China and India." *Development Forum* 13 (10): 3–4.

King, F. H.
1927   *Farmers of Forty Centuries, or Permanent Agriculture in China, Korea and Japan*. New York: Harcourt, Brace.

Kirby, E. Stuart
1960   *Rural Progress in Taiwan*. Taibei: Chinese-American Joint Commission on Rural Reconstruction.

Kirkby, R. J. R.
1985   *Urbanization in China: Town and Country in a Developing Economy 1949–2000 A.D.* New York: Columbia University Press.

Knapp, Ronald G.
1976   "Chinese Frontier Settlement in Taiwan." *Annals, Association of American Geographers* 66 (1): 43–59.
1977   "The Changing Landscape of the Chinese Cemetery." *The China Geographer* 8:1–13.
1980   "Settlement and Frontier Land Tenure." In Ronald G. Knapp, ed., *China's Island Frontier: Studies in the Historical Geography of Taiwan*, pp. 55–68. Honolulu: The University Press of Hawaii.
1982a   "Chinese Rural Dwellings in Taiwan." *Journal of Cultural Geography* 3 (1): 1–18.

1982b   "Chinese Vernacular Burial." *Orientations* 13 (7): 28–33.

Kokubu Naoichi and Shioji Etsusaburo
1954   "Taihoku bonchi ni okeru binzokukei noko shu to shite jukyo no kochiku, kozo, setsubi, pi tsuite" [The farmhouses of the Formosan Chinese in the Taibei basin]. *Minzokugaku-kenkyu* [Japanese journal of ethnology] 18 (1/2): 161–178.

Kuo Li-cheng
1973   "House Building Hexes." *Echo* 3 (11): 40–46.

Lamley, Harry
1981   "Subethnic Rivalry in the Ch'ing Period." In Emily Martin Ahern and Hill Gates, eds., *The Anthropology of Taiwanese Society*, pp. 282–318. Stanford: Stanford University Press.

Lee Chien-lang [Li Qianlang]
1977   "The An Tai Lin Family House." *Echo* 6 (6): 18–25.
1978   *Jinmen minju jianzhu* [A survey of Jinmen (Kinmen) traditional architecture]. Taibei: Xiongshi tushu gongsi.
1980   *Taiwan jianzhu shi* [History of the architecture of Taiwan]. Taibei: Beiwu chubanshe.

Li Chengrui
1985   "Economic Reform Brings Better Life." *Beijing Review* 28 (29): 15–22. July 22.

Li Chengrui and Zhang Zhongji
1982   "Remarkable Improvements in Living Standards." *Beijing Review* 25 (17): 15–18, 28. April 26.

Li Chengzu
1984   "Chengzhen fangwu pucha jiang quanmian zhankai" [A survey of housing in cities and towns will be comprehensively carried out]. *Renmin ribao* [People's daily]. July 30.

Li Yun
1982   "Develop New Style Building Materials According to Local Need." *Jingji guanli* [Economic management] 3:37–40.

Liang Sicheng [Liang Ssu-ch'eng]
1981   *Zhongguo jianzhushi* [A history of Chinese architecture]. Taibei: Wenshuju gufen youxian gongsi [reprint of 1955 Shangwu yinshuguan edition].
1983   *Yingzao fashi zhufan* [Explanation of the *Yingzao fashi*]. Beijing: Zhongguo jianzhu gongye chubanshe.

Liang Ssu-ch'eng [Liang Sicheng]
1984   Edited by Wilma Fairbank. *A Pictorial History of*

Chinese Architecture: A Study of the Development of Its Structural System and the Evolution of Its Types. Cambridge: MIT Press.

Lin Hengdao [Lin Heng-tao]
1960   "Taiwan gulao de zhuzhai" [The old houses of Taiwan]. *Taiwan fengwu* [Taiwan folkways] 21 (2): 35–41.
1975   "Taiwan's Traditional Chinese Houses." *Echo* 5 (11): 23–27, 54, 56.

Lin Senmu, Zhou Shulian, and Qi Mingchen
1984   "Industry and Transport." In Yu Guangyuan, ed., *China's Socialist Modernization*, pp. 271–349. Beijing: Foreign Languages Press.

Liu Chenlie
1980   "New Rural Homes." *China Reconstructs* 29 (9): 16–17.

Liu Dizhong
1984   "State Plans to Reduce Rural Fuel Shortages." *China Daily* 4 (959): 1. August 22.

Liu Dunzhen
1957   *Zhongguo zhuzhai gaishuo* [Introduction to Chinese dwellings]. Beijing: Jianzhu gongcheng chubanshe.

Liu Dunzhen, ed.
1980   *Zhongguo gudai jianzhu shi* [History of ancient Chinese architecture]. Beijing: Zhongguo jianzhu gongye chubanshe.
1984   *Zhongguo gudai jianzhu shi, di er ban* [History of ancient Chinese architecture, 2nd ed.]. Beijing: Zhongguo jianzhu gongye chubanshe.

Liu Songtau and Zhu Bizhen, eds.
1983   *Nongcun zhuzhai fangantu* [Plans for rural houses]. Tianjin: Tianjin kexue jishu chubanshe.

Liu Zhiping
1957   *Zhongguo jianzhu leixing ji jiegou* [Chinese architectural types and structural forms]. Beijing: Jianzhu gongcheng chubanshe.

Lu Yuanding
1978   "Nanfang diqu chuantong jianzhu de tongfeng yu fangre" [The ventilation and heat insulation of traditional architecture in south China]. *Jianzhu xuebao* [Architectural journal] 4: 36–41.

Ma, Laurence J. C.
1981   "Urban Housing Supply in the People's Republic of China." In Laurence J. C. Ma and Edward W. Hanten, eds., *Urban Development in Modern China*, pp. 222–259. Boulder: Westview Press.

March, Andrew
1968   "An Appreciation of Chinese Geomancy." *Journal of Asian Studies* 27:253–267.

Myrdal, Jan
1965   *Report from a Chinese Village.* New York: New American Library.

Needham, Joseph
1956   *Science and Civilisation in China.* Vol. 2, *History of Scientific Thought.*
1971   Vol. 4, *Physics and Physical Technology.* Cambridge: Cambridge University Press.

Nie Lisheng
1985   "Farmland Drain Spurs State Law." *China Daily* 5 (1282): 3. September 2.

Qi Yingtao
1981   *Zeyang jianding gujianzhu* [How to identify traditional architecture]. Beijing: n.p.

Raper, Arthur
1953   *Rural Taiwan—Problem and Prospect.* Taibei: Chinese-American Joint Commission on Rural Reconstruction.

Rapoport, Amos
1969   *House Form and Culture.* Englewood Cliffs: Prentice-Hall.

"Rural Construction Receives State Aid"
1985   *China Daily* 5 (1245): 2. July 22.

"Rural Housing Boom"
1981   *Beijing Review* 24 (21): 7. May 25.

"Sample Survey of Peasant Household Incomes and Expenditures"
1983   *Beijing Review* 26 (43): 22–23. October 24.

Seaman, Gary
1985   Personal communication. October 5.

Shan Deqi
1984   "Cunxi, tianjing, matouqiang—Huizhou minju biji" [Village streams, courtyards, gable walls—notes on the vernacular architecture of Huizhou]. *Jianzhu shi lunwenji* [Treatise on the history of architecture] 6:120–134.

Shan Shiyuan
1981   "Hangtu jishu qiantan" [Summary talk on the earth tamping technique]. *Keji shi wenji* [Collection on the history of science and technology] 7:119–123.

Shima Yukio
1940   *Manshu-koku min-oku chiri* [A geography of private houses in Manchuria]. Tokyo: Kokon Sho-in.

"Shortages of Housing Yet to Be Eased"
1985   *China Daily* 4(1197): 4. May 5.

Shuzo Shiga
1978   "Family Property and the Law of Inheritance in Traditional China." In David C. Buxbaum, ed., *Chinese Family Law and Social Change in Historical Perspective*, pp. 109–150. Seattle: University of Washington Press.

Smil, Vaclav
1984   *The Bad Earth: Environmental Degradation in China.* Armonk, N.Y.: M.E. Sharpe.

"Solving the Problem of Urban Housing"
1985   *China Daily* 5 (1344): 4. November 13.

Song Yingxing [Sung Ying-hsing]
1978   *Tiangong kaiwu* [The creations of nature and man]. Annotated by Zhong Guangyan. Hong Kong: Zhonghua shuju.

Spencer, Joseph
1947   "The Houses of the Chinese." *Geographical Review* 37:254–273.

Steinhardt, Nancy Shatzman
1984a   "Bracketing System of the Song Dynasty." In Nancy Shatzman Steinhardt, ed., *Chinese Traditional Architecture,* pp. 121–125. New York: China Institute in America.

Steinhardt, Nancy Shatzman, ed.
1984b   *Chinese Traditional Architecture.* New York: China Institute in America.

Sung Ying-hsing [Song Yingxing]
1966   *T'ien-kung k'ai-wu: Chinese Technology in the Seventeenth Century.* Translated by E-tu Zen Sun and Shiou-chuan Sun. University Park: Pennsylvania University Press.

Swinhoe, Robert
1859   "Narrative of a Visit to the Island of Formosa." *Journal of the North China Branch, Royal Geographic Society* 2:1–164.

Taiwanfu zhi [Gazetteer of Taiwan *fu*]
1761   Reissued as *Taiwan wenxian congkan, di 65 zhong.* Taibei: Taiwan yinhang, 1960.

Tao Ji
1984   "Jianzhu kaogu sanshinian zongshu" [Survey of the architectural archaelogy of the past 30 years]. *Jianzhu lishi yu lilun* [Corpus of architectural history and theory], 3/4:13–52.

Thomson, J.
1873   "Notes of a Journey in Southern Formosa." *Journal of the Royal Geographic Society* 43:97–107.

Thorp, Robert L.
1983   "Origins of Chinese Architectural Style: The Earliest Plans and Building Types." *Archives of Asian Art* 36:22–39.

"Tianjin Opens Model Rural Homes"
1985   *China Daily* 4 (1119): 1. February 25.

Tuan, Yi-fu
1969   *China.* Chicago: Aldine.

von Poseck, Helena
1905   "How John Chinaman Builds His House." *East of Asia Magazine* 4:348–355.

Waley, Arthur, trans.
1937   *The Book of Songs.* New York: Grove Press.

Wang Guixin
1984   "Tantao jieyue jiben jianshe yongdi de tujing" [An exploration of ways to save land in capital construction]. *Jianzhu xuebao* [Architectural journal] 11:50–53, 36.

Wang, Sung-hsing
1971   "Pooling and Sharing in a Chinese Fishing Economy: Kueishan Tao." Ph.D. dissertation, University of Tokyo.
1974   "Taiwanese Architecture and the Supernatural." In Arthur P. Wolf, ed., *Religion and Ritual in Chinese Society*, pp. 183–192. Stanford: Stanford University Press.

Wang Zhunrong
1882   *Yangzhai shishu* [Ten writings on *yang* dwellings]. Beijing?: Shanchengtang cangban.

Wenwu cankao ziliao [Cultural relics research material]
1954   9:140.

Wheatley, Paul
1971   *The Pivot of the Four Quarters: A Preliminary Inquiry into the Origins and Character of the Ancient Chinese City.* Chicago: Aldine.

Wolf, Arthur P.
1981   "Domestic Organization." In Emily Martin Ahern and Hill Gates, eds., *The Anthropology of Taiwanese Society,* pp. 341–360. Stanford: Stanford University Press.

Wright, Arthur F.
1965   "Symbolism and Function: Reflections on Changan and Other Great Cities." *Journal of Asian Studies* 24 (4): 667–679.
1977   "The Cosmology of the Chinese City." In G. William Skinner, ed., *The City in Late Imperial China,* pp. 33–73. Stanford: Stanford University Press.

Xian Banpo buowuguan [Banpo Museum, Xian], ed.
1982   *Xian Banpo* [Neolithic site at Banpo near Xian]. Xian: Wenwu chubanshe.

Xiao Tihuan
1985   "Woguo cunzhen jianshe jiakuai mianmao gaiguan" [Increasing changes in the face of construction in the nation's villages and towns]. *Renmin ribao—haiwaiban* [People's daily—overseas edition] 1. November 8.

Xinhua zidian [New Chinese dictionary]
1984   Beijing: Shangwu yinshuguan.

Xu Yuanchao
1985   "Construction Plan to Ease Urban Housing Shortage." *China Daily* 5 (1356): 1. November 27.

Xu Zhengzhong
1985   "Woguo nongmin xiaofei shuiping xunsu tigao" [Consumption levels of the nation's peasants rise rapidly]. *Renmin ribao—haiwaiban* [People's daily—overseas edition] 1. November 6.

Yang Hongxun
1980a   "Hemudu yizhi mugou shuijing jianding ji caoqi mugou gongyi kaucha" [Identification of the timber structure well at the Hemudu ruins and inspection of the technology of timber structure during the early period]. *Keji shi wenji* [Collection on the history of science and technology] 5:63–70.
1980b   "Zhongguo caoqi jianzhu de fazhan" [The development of early architecture in China]. *Jianzhu lishi yu lilun* [Corpus of architectural history and theory] 1:112–135.

Yu Guangyuan, ed.
1984   *China's Socialist Modernization.* Beijing: Foreign Languages Press.

Yu Ling
1985   "A Rural World of Stone." *China Daily* 5 (1360): 6. December 2.

Zai Junfu
1984   "Adobe Architecture" lecture at Qinghua University, Beijing.

Zhan Wu and Liu Wenpu
1984   "Agriculture." In Yu Guangyuan, ed., *China's Socialist Modernization,* pp. 207–270. Beijing: Foreign Languages Press.

Zhang Naihua
1985   "Putting Rural China on Tap." *South* 60 (11): 178–179.

Zhang Zhongyi et al.
1957   *Huizhou Mingdai zhuzhai* [Ming dynasty houses in Huizhou]. Beijing: Jianzhu gongcheng chubanshe.

Zhao Bonian
1983   "Rural Housing Boom: New Designs for Changing Lifestyles." *China Reconstructs* 32 (3): 52–56.

Zhao Ziyang
1983   "Report on the Sixth Five-Year Plan." In *Fifth Session of the Fifth National People's Congress (Main Documents).* Beijing: Foreign Languages Press.

"Zhejiang Rehouses Farmers"
1985   *China Daily* 5 (1334): 3. November 1.

Zhongguo jianzhu jishu fazhan zhongxin, jianzhu lishi yanjiusuo [Center for Chinese Architectural Technology Development, Research Unit for Architectural History].
1984   *Zhejiang minju* [The folk houses of Zhejiang]. Beijing: Zhongguo jianzhu gongye chubanshe.

Zhongguo jianzhu kexue yanjiuyuan, nongcun jianzhu yanjiusuo [Institute of Chinese Architectural Science, research unit for rural architecture]
1982   *1981 nian quanguo nongcun zhuzhai sheji jingsai youshou fangan xuanbian* [Selection of outstanding proposals from the 1981 national rural housing design competition]. Beijing: Zhongguo jianzhu kexue yanjiuyuan.

Zhongguo wenhua xueyuan, jianzhu xuehui [College of Chinese Culture, Architectural Society], eds.
1974   "Taiwan de chuantong jianzhu" [The traditional architecture of Taiwan]. *Taiwan fengwu* [Taiwan folkways] 24 (1): 35–61.

Zhou Zhongxuan
1717   *Zhulo xianzhi* [Zhulo *xian* gazetteer]. Reissued as *Taiwan yanjiu congkan, di 55 zhong.* Taibei: Taiwan yinhang, 1958.

Zhu Ling
1986   "New House Construction Soars with Rural Boom." *China Daily* 5(1411): 1 January 31.

Zhuang Jinde
1964   "Qingchu yanjin yanhai renmin toudu lai Tai shimo" [History of the early Qing prohibition against coastal people's illegal crossing to Taiwan]. *Taiwan wenxian* [Taiwan documents] 15 (3): 1–20; 15 (4): 40–62.

FURTHER REFERENCES

Ahern, Emily
1979   "Domestic Architecture in Taiwan: Continuity and Change." In Richard W. Wilson, Amy Auerbacker Wilson, and Sidney L. Greenblatt, eds., *Value Change in Chinese Society,* pp. 155–170. New York: Praeger.

Ahern, Emily and Hill Gates
1981   *The Anthropology of Taiwanese Society.* Stanford: Stanford University Press.

Anonymous
1979   "La maison traditionnelle des provinces du nord et du nord-est." *L'architecture d'aujourdhui* 201:74–77.

Arnaiz, Gregorio
1910   "Construccion de los edificios en las prefecturas de Coan-ciu y Cian-ciu, Fu-kien sur, China." *Anthropos* 5:907–933.

Baker-Carr, Kay
1951   "The Chinese House." *Journal of the Royal Architectural Institute of Canada* 5:234–235.

Blazer, Werner
1979   *Hofhaus in China: Tradition und Gegenwart.* Basel: Birkhauser.

Cen Shuhuan
1956   "Guangdong zhongbu yanhai diqu de minjian jianzhu" [Folk architecture in the coastal areas of Guangdong province]. *Jianzhu xuebao* [Architectural journal] 2:36–46.

Chatfield-Taylor, Adele
1981   "Vernacular Architecture and Historic Preservation in Modern China." *Ekistics* 288:199–201.

Chen Tainong
1975   *Tainanqu nongcun zhuzhai jianzhu zhi yanjiu* [Research on the construction of rural dwellings in the Tainan area]. Tainan: Yuning chuban youxian gongsi.

Chinese Academy of Architecture
1982   *Ancient Chinese Architecture.* Beijing and Hong Kong: Joint Publications Company.

Chow, Renee Y.
1980   "People's Places: Public Spatial Structure in Chinese Villages." Thesis, Department of Architecture, Massachusetts Institute of Technology.

Cressey, George B.
1932   "Chinese Homes and Homesites." *Home Geographic Monthly* 2 (3): 31–36.

Dai Fudong
1984   "Guizhou yanshi jianzhu" [Rock construction in Guizhou]. *Jianzhushi* [The architect] 20:80–90.

Dai Yannian
1985   "Jiangsu Villagers Show Off the Future." *Beijing Review* 28 (30): 17–20. July 29.

Dudgeon, John
1884   "Diet, Dress, and Dwellings of the Chinese in Relation to Health." *International Health Exhibition, London, 1884. The Health Exhibition Literature.* London: William Clowes & Sons.

Eitel, E. J.
1873   *Fengshui or the Rudiments of Natural Science in China.* London: Trubner.

Fujishima Gaijiro
1948   *Taiwan no kenchiku* [The architecture of Taiwan].
        Tokyo: Shokoku-sha.

Fuller, Myron L. and Frederick G. Clapp
1924   "Loess and Rock Dwellings of Shensi, China."
        Geographical Review 14:215–226.

Gu Baohe et al.
1982   "Nongjia le: nongcun zhuzhai jianzhu tixi"
        [The happy peasant family: the rural housing
        system]. *Jianzhu xuebao* [Architectural journal]
        10:59–61.

Guo Daiheng
1981   "Lun Zhongguo gudai mugou jianzhu de mou-
        shuzhi" [Modular systems in Chinese tradi-
        tional architecture]. *Jianzhu shi lunwenji* [Trea-
        tise on the history of architecture] 5:31–47.

Huang Baoyu
1973   *Zhongguo jianzhu shi* [A history of Chinese archi-
        tecture]. Taibei: Zhengzhong shuju yinhang.

Huang Yu-mei
1983a   "Presto! A 'New' Ancient Landmark." *Free
        China Review* 34 (8): 56–63.
1983b   "South China Is Reborn in Taiwan's Newest
        Old Village." *Free China Review* 33 (12): 67–73.

Inn, Henry
1940   *Chinese Houses and Gardens*. New York: Bonanza
        Books.

Izikowitz, K. G. and P. Sorensen, eds.
1982   *The House in East and Southeast Asia: Anthropologi-
        cal and Architectural Aspects*. Scandinavian Insti-
        tute of Asian Studies Monograph Series No.
        30. London: Curzon Press.

Jiangsu sheng jianzhu anzhuang gongcheng gongsi nong-
gongcuo zu [Rural Housing Working Group of the
Jiangsu Provincial Engineering Company]
1966   "Shizhi tuiguang shuini goujian, jiji zhihuan
        nongmin jianfang" [Trial popularization of
        concrete structural components, a positive aid
        in the construction of peasants' homes]. *Jianzhu
        xuebao* [Architectural journal] 1:27–31.

Jin Obo
1962   "Dui dangqian nongcun zhuzhai shejizhang
        jige wenti de tantao" [A study of some prob-
        lems of recent rural housing design]. *Jianzhu
        xuebao* 9:4–8.

Klatt, W.
1983   "The Staff of Life: Living Standards in China,
        1977–1981." *China Quarterly* 93:17–50.

Knapp, Ronald G.
1981   "Taiwan's Vernacular Architecture." *Orienta-
        tions* 12 (4): 38–47.

Lancaster, Clay
1950   "The Origin and Formation of Chinese Archi-
        tecture." *Journal of the Society of Architectural Histo-
        rians* 9 (1/4): 3–10.

Lee, Tunney
1982   "The Changing Countryside." *Mimar: Architec-
        ture in Development* 3:25–27.

Li Jiafu
1977   *Zhongguo gudai jianzhu yishu* [The art and archi-
        tecture of ancient China]. Taibei: Beiwu chu-
        banshiye gufen youxian gongsi.

Liang Sicheng wenji-yi [Collected works of Liang Sicheng:
vol. 1]
1982   Beijing: Zhongguo jianzhu gongye chubanshe.

Lin Hengdao [Lin Heng-tao]
1963   "Taibeishi de guxian zhuzhai" [The old houses
        of Taibei]. *Taibei wenxian* [Documents of Taibei]
        3:75–102.

Lip, Evelyn
1979   *Chinese Geomancy*. Singapore: Times Books In-
        ternational.

Liu Dunzhen wenji-yi [Collected works of Liu Dunzhen:
vol. 1]
1982   Beijing: Zhongguo jianzhu gongye chubanshe.

Liu Dunzhen wenji-er [Collected works of Liu Dunzhen:
vol. 2]
1984   Beijing: Zhongguo jianzhu gongye chubanshe.

Liu Yixing
1983   "Taiwan jianzhu tedian qianxi" [Characteris-
        tics of architecture in Taiwan]. *Jianzhu xuebao*
        [Architectural journal] 2:68–70.

Loewe, Michael
1981   "China." In Michael Loewe and Carmen
        Blacker, eds., *Oracles and Divination*, pp. 38–62.
        Boulder: Shambhala.

Lu Shu
1975   "Woguo gudai de nenggong qiaojiang—Lu
        Ban" [A skilled craftsman from the past—Lu
        Ban]. *Jianzhu xuebao* [Architectural journal]
        1:16.

Lu Yuanding and Wei Yanjun
1982   "Guangdong Huxian minju" [Folk housing of
        Huxian, Guangdong]. *Jianzhushi* [The archi-
        tect] 13:141–162.

Lu Yuchun [Lu Yu-tsun]
1971   *Zhongguo jianzhu shi yu Yingzao fashi* [Chinese architecture and the *Yingzao fashi*]. Taibei: Zhongguo wenhua xueyuan jianzhu ji dushi jihua xueshe chuban.

Luccioni, Xavier
1979   "Des architectures de la campagne." *L'architecture d'aujourdhui* 201:68–73.

Penn, Colin
1965   "Chinese Vernacular Architecture." *Journal of the Royal Institute of British Architects* 72 (10): 502–507.

Pezeu-Massabuau, Jacques
1969   "Les problemes geographiques de la maison chinoise." *Cahiers d'outre mer: Revue de geographie de Bordeaux et de l'Atlantique* 22 (87): 252–287.

Pirazzoli-T'Sertstevens, Michele
1971   *Living Architecture: Chinese.* New York: Grosset & Dunlap.

"Restoration of Lin An-tai Mansion Set"
1984   *Free China Journal* 1 (33): 3. August 19.

Richardson, David B.
1977   "Sino-Japanese and Contemporary Architecture: Philosophical Influences and Parallels." *Chinese Culture* 18 (4): 19–31.

Rong Yen
1980   "The 'Square Courtyard' of Old Beijing." *China Reconstructs* 29 (9): 15–16.

Rossbach, Sarah
1983   *Feng Shui: The Chinese Art of Placement.* New York: E. P. Dutton.

Rural Architecture in Hong Kong
1979   Hong Kong: Government Information Services.

Schmertz, Mildred F.
1982   "Islamic Architecture and Rural Dwellings from Beijing to Kashi." *Architectural Record* 170:92–101.

Shan Deqi
1980   "Sichuan difang jianzhu caifeng" [Vernacular architecture of Sichuan province]. *Jianzhu shi lunwenji* [Treatise on the history of architecture] 4:85–92.

Shan Shiyuan
1981   "Zhongguo wuwa de fazhan guocheng shitan" [Tentative research into the development of Chinese roof tiles]. *Jianzhu lishi yu lilun* [Corpus of architectural history and theory] 2:1–4.

Shan Yu
1980   "New Materials for Home Building." *China Reconstructs* 29 (7): 48–49.

Shang Kuo
1980   "Minju—xin jianzhu chuangcuo de zhongyao cuojian" [Housing—important experience for designing new buildings]. *Jianzhu lishi yu lilun* [History and theory of architecture] 1:86–103.

Shang Kuo and Yang Lingyu
1982   "Chuantong tingyuanshi zhuzhai yu diceng gao midu" [The traditional courtyard-style dwelling and the high density of low buildings]. *Jianzhu xuebao* [Architectural journal] 5:51–60.

Shen Chenzhong and Wang Fugui
1981   "An Investigation into Problems of Rural Housing in Suburban Shanghai." *Nongye jingji wenti* [Problems of agricultural economics] 6:54–55.

Skinner, R. T. F.
1958   "Chinese Domestic Architecture." *Journal of the Royal Institute of British Architects* 65:430–431.

Skinner, Stephen
1982   *The Living Earth Manual of Feng-Shui.* London: Routledge & Kegan Paul.

Soper, Alexander
1956   "Architecture." In Lawrence Sickman and Alexander Soper, *The Art and Architecture of China,* pp. 205–320. Middlesex: Harmondsworth.

Su Gin-djih (Xu Jingzhi)
1964   *Chinese Architecture—Past and Contemporary.* Hong Kong: Sin Poh Amalgamated.

Sullivan, Linda F.
1972   "Traditional Chinese Regional Architecture: Chinese Houses." *Journal of the Royal Asiatic Society of Great Britain and Ireland, Hong Kong Branch* 12:131–149.

Sun, Paul
1982   "Underground Houses." *Mimar: Architecture in Development* 3:41–46.
1984   "*Feng-shui:* The Science Behind the Belief." Unpublished manuscript.

Tao Tsung-chen
1965   "Chinese Roof Styles." *Canadian Architect* 77:70–72.

Thilo, Thomas
1977   *Klassische chinesische Baukunst: Strukturprinzipien und Sozial Funktion.* Leipzig: Koehler & Amelang.

Wang, Betty
  1983   "The Complex Engineering of China's Archi-
          tectural Treasures." *Free China Review* 34 (7):
          64–71.

Wang Jiafeng
  1983   "Zhongguo chuantong jianzhu de guanmian"
          [The high point of Chinese architecture].
          Guanghua [Sinorama] 8:52–58.

Wang, Mei
  1976   "The Practice of Architecture in the People's
          Republic of China since 1949." Thesis, Depart-
          ment of Architecture, Massachusetts Institute
          of Technology.

Wang Shaozhou
  1980   "Beijing siheyuan zhuzhai de zucheng yu gou-
          zao" [The composition and structure of the
          courtyard dwellings of Beijing]. *Keji shi wenji*
          [Collection on the history of science and tech-
          nology] 5:92–101.

Wang Zhongshu
  1982   *Han Civilization.* New Haven: Yale University
          Press.

Wiens, Herold
  1954   *China's March to the Tropics.* Hamden, Conn.:
          Shoestring Press.

Wolf, Margery
  1968   *The House of Lim.* New York: Appleton-Cen-
          tury-Crofts.

Wu Deyao
  1982   "Wuxian weixingdadui jumin dian guihua ji
          sheyuan zhuzhai" [The residential planning
          and houses of Weixing production brigade in
          Wuxian]. *Jianzhu xuebao* [Architectural journal]
          4:64–67.

Wu, Nelson
  1963   *Chinese and Indian Architecture: The City of Man,
          the Mountain of God, and the Realm of the Immortals.*
          New York: George Braziller.

Wu Yongzhen
  1980   "Fengjian guannian he jiude chuantong xiguan
          cai jianzhuzhong de fanying" [The reflection of
          feudal ideas and old traditional behavior in ar-
          chitecture]. *Jianzhu xuebao* [Architectural jour-
          nal] 3:34–35.

Wu Zhongwei
  1950   *Fangwu jianzhuxue* [The architecture of dwell-
          ings]. Hong Kong: Haijiao tushu wenju you-
          xian gongsi.

Xin Wen
  1984   "The Remains of a 7,000-Year-Old Society at
          Hemudu Village." In *Recent Discoveries in Chinese
          Archaeology,* pp. 8–10. Beijing: Foreign Lan-
          guages Press.

Yan Zheng
  1981   "Tianjing zhuzhai wenti tantao" [A discussion
          of light wells in residences]. *Jianzhu xuebao* [Ar-
          chitectural journal] 5:64–67.

Yang Hongxun
  1981a   "Dougong qiyuan kaocha" [Investigation of
          the origin of the *dougong*]. *Jianzhu lishi yu lilun*
          [Corpus of architectural history and theory]
          2:5–16.
  1981b   "Shilun Zhongguo huangtu didai jieyue neng-
          yuan de dixia jumin dian" [An examination of
          the economizing of resources in the folk dwell-
          ings of China's loessial region]. *Jianzhu xuebao*
          [Architectural journal] 5:68–73.

Yetts, Perceval
  1927   "Writings on Chinese Architecture." *Burlington
          Magazine* 50:116–131.

Yin-yang dili fengshui chuanji [A complete collection on *fengshui*]
  1975   Yonghe, Taiwan: Dafang chubanshe.

Yoshiro Tomita
  1936   "To no sonaku kyoju keikan no hikaku" [Com-
          parison of the settlements and dwellings of
          south China and Taiwan]. *Taiwan jiho* [Taiwan
          times] 194:37–42.
  1943   "Taiwan minka no kenkyu" [The form of resi-
          dences in Taiwan]. *Minzoku Taiwan* [The eth-
          nology of Taiwan] 3 (1): 2–9.

Yu Zhuoyun
  1980   "Dougong de yunyong shi woguo gudai jian-
          zhu jishu de zhongyao gongxian" [Application
          of *dougong* in ancient Chinese buildings was an
          important contribution to architectural technol-
          ogy]. *Keji shi wenji* [Collection on the history of
          science and technology] 5:40–62.

Zhang Jingxian
  1980   "Feiyan yinjiao, xia" [Flying eaves, pt. 2].
          Jianzhu shi lunwenji [Treatise on the history of
          architecture] 4:67–84.

Zhang Wenrui
  1977   "Zhongguo minju de fazhan he shigong fang-
          fa" [Development and methods of construction
          of Chinese dwellings]. Thesis, Zhongguo wen-
          hua xueyuan, Taibei.

Zhang Yuhuan
  1980   "Wo guo gudai jianzhu cailiao de fazhan ji qi
          chengjiu" [Development and achievement of
          building materials in ancient China]. *Jianzhu
          lishi yu lilun* [Corpus of architectural history and
          theory] 1:186–191.

Zhao Jizhu
  1984   "Jiantan Zhongguo gudai jianzhu shigong
          gongju" [Brief discussion of the tools used in
          ancient Chinese architecture]. *Keji shi wenji*
          [Collection on the history of science and tech-
          nology] 11:153–164.

Zhao Zhengzhi
  1964   "Zhongguo gu jianzhu gongcheng jishu"
          [Building technology in ancient China]. *Jianzhu
          shi lunwenji* [Treatise on the history of architec-
          ture] 1:10–33.

ILLUSTRATION CREDITS

Yang Hongxun (1980b): 1.1, 1.2

Xian Banpo buowuguan (1982): 1.3, 1.4, 1.5

Ronald G. Knapp: 1.6, 2.1, 2.2, 2.3, 2.4, 2.5, 2.6, 2.7, 2.9, 2.10, 2.14, 2.15, 2.16, 2.20, 2.21, 2.22, 2.23, 2.27, 2.28, 2.30, 2.40, 2.41, 2.42, 3.1, 3.3, 3.4, 3.5, 3.6, 3.7, 3.8, 3.13, 3.14, 3.15, 3.16, 3.17, 3.18, 3.19, 3.20, 3.21, 3.22, 3.23, 3.24, 3.25, 3.27, 3.28, 3.29, 3.31, 3.35, 3.38, 3.39, 3.45, 3.46, 3.48, 3.53, 3.56, 3.60, 4.2, 4.3, 4.4, 4.11, 4.14, 4.15, 5.4, 5.8, 5.9, 6.3, 6.4, 6.5, 6.6, 6.7, 6.9, 6.11, 6.12, 6.18, 6.19, 6.20, 6.21, 6.22, 6.23, 6.24, 6.25. Plates 1, 3, 4, 5, 6, 7, 9, 10, 11, 12, 13

Liu Dunzhen (1984): 1.7, 1.10, 1.11, 1.12

Guangzhou shi wenwu guanli weiyuanhui (1958): 1.8

Wenwu cankao ziliao (1954): 1.9

Zhang Zhongyi et al. (1957): 1.13

Arthur J. Van Alstyne: 2.8, 2.17, 2.18, 2.24, 2.29, 3.10, 3.11, 3.12, 3.57, 3.61, 6.8. Plates 2, 8

Shima Yukio (1940): 2.11, 2.12

Beijing shi jianshe shejiyuan (1962): 2.13

Paul Sun: 2.19, 2.25, 2.26

Gao Zhenming, Yang Daoming, Chen Yu (1983): 2.31

Huang Hanmin: 2.32, 2.33, 2.35, 2.36, 2.37

Liu Dunzhen (1957): 2.34, 2.38, 2.39, 3.33, 3.34, 3.44, 3.47, 3.50, 3.51, 3.58

Joseph Needham (1971): 3.2

Song Yingxing (1978): 3.9, 3.54, 3.59

Zhongguo jianzhu jishu fazhan zhongxin (1984): 3.26, 3.40, 3.41, 3.43

Xinhua Zidian (1984): 3.37

Liu Zhiping (1957): 3.49

Deng Qisheng (1980): 3.55

Zhou Zhongxuan (1717): 4.1

Lee Chien-lang (1980): 4.5, 4.12, 4.16

Huang Yu-mei (1983): 4.6

Kokubu Naoichi and Shioji Etsusaburo (1954): 4.7

Lawrence Crissman: 4.8, 4.10

Leonard H. D. Gordon: 4.9

Joseph Needham (1956): 5.1

Dixue tanyuan (1966): 5.2

Wang Zhunrong (1882): 5.3

Guang Jing Tang (1975): 5.5

Henry Dore (1917–1918): 5.6

Lu Ban jing jiangjia jing, after Kuo (1973): 5.7

V. R. Burkhardt (1955): 5.10

Jiang Zhengrong et al. (1984): 6.1, 6.2

Gao Shangde and Zeng Hujiu (1982): 6.10

Zhao Bonian (1983): 6.13

Zhongguo jianzhu kexue yanjiuyuan (1982): 6.14, 6.15, 6.16, 6.17

INDEX

References to illustrations are in boldface

ABOUT THE AUTHOR

Ronald G. Knapp is professor of geography at the State University of New York, College at New Paltz. In addition to editing and contributing to *China's Island Frontier: Studies in the Historical Geog-* *raphy of Taiwan,* he has published numerous articles on the historical and cultural geography of China.

▦ Production Notes

This book was designed by Roger Eggers. Composition and paging were done on the Quadex Composing System and typesetting on the Compugraphic 8400 by the design and production staff of University of Hawaii Press.

The text typeface is Baskerville and the display typeface is Compugraphic Palatino.

Offset presswork and binding were done by Vail-Ballou Press, Inc. Text paper is Glatco coated matte, basis 60.